the art of conversation

Hugh Gyton
with Tracey Ward

Second Edition

First Published 2007
Second Edition 2015

© Copyright 2007 Hugh Gyton

All rights reserved. No part of this book may be reproduced or transmitted in any form by any means, electronic or mechanical, including photocopying, recording or by any information storage or retrieval system, without the written permission in writing from the publisher. The Australian Copyright Act 1968 (the Act) allows a maximum of one chapter or 10 per cent of the book, whichever is the greater, to be photocopied by any educational institution for its educational purposes provided that the educational institution (or body that administers it) has given a remuneration notice to Copyright Agency Limited (CAL) under the Act.

Gyton, Hugh.

The art of conversation

ISBN 9780980408713 (pbk.).

1. Conversation. 2. Body Language. 3. Interpersonal communication. 4. Interpersonal relations. 5. Oral communication. I. Ward, Tracey. II. Title. (Series: Just a conversation).

Project managed by Hugh Gyton & Associates
www.hughgyton.com

In loving memory of Peggy and Katie.

Contents

Acknowledgements

Introduction

1	What is conversation?	1
2	Say	21
3	Do	37
4	Think	53
5	Conversation M.O.D.E.™	67
6	Building rapport	81
7	Body language	97
8	First impressions	111
9	Advanced conversation techniques	125
10	Other forms of conversation	135

Endnotes 151

Acknowledgements

With thanks to my mother who all those years ago started me on this journey, literally and figuratively. The patient hours you spent in inspiring conversation in my formative years laid the foundation for what has now become my passion.

To my co-parent, friend and co-author; Tracey without whom this book would not have been written. Thank you for teaching me the gift of open, honest communication and the skill of not taking myself too seriously.

Special mention for my two beautiful children, Baxby and Serta, who daily teach me lessons in 'the art of conversation' and bring so much love and laughter into our lives.

For my friends and clients who share, support, and converse with me on a daily basis.

Introduction

Have you ever noticed some people just seem to be in the right place at the right time? They get the cool job, the promotion, the gorgeous girl or the handsome guy, the free tickets, the party invites ... need I go on?

Do you know someone like this?

People like this appear to be extremely lucky. But are they?

When you look at these lucky people objectively, you might admit that they are not necessarily better at their job, nor are they necessarily more attractive than you. Nor are they necessarily a 'better' person – yet opportunities seem to evolve around them, and people flock to them.

So just what is it that they do differently?

Of course there could be numerous factors involved. However one thing is for certain – they will all be good at conversation. That is, they are good at *making their conversations work properly for them*. Their strong conversation skills will enable them to quickly build rapport with new contacts, easily develop strong relationships, have greater success in getting what they want and always get their intended message across the right way, reducing the potential for misunderstandings and conflict.

Want to learn their secrets?

As a conversations expert, I have many years of experience working with people on developing just these skills. My clients have held different roles and worked in different organisations, and I've worked with them for different reasons. Some of them need help in building up rather ordinary conversational skills, and others just want to polish or fine-tune their abilities. Regardless of who I'm working with, though, I give each of my clients three things to think about:

1. The words they choose to use, and how they deliver those words (what they say)

2. How well they focus on their conversations, how open they are to conversations, and how their attitude to the person they're talking to helps or hinders them (what they think)

3. The physical nature of their responses to the other person while talking to them: their body language, facial expressions, and even their choice of location and the timing of each conversation (what they do).

Strengthening these three conversational threads of *say*, *think*, and *do* helps to create compelling connections with others, in every conversational situation.

This book is full of practical tips to help you avoid the pitfalls and enhance your conversation skills, and it will help you become clearer and more believable in all your conversations.

It is not necessarily rocket science or that latest 'how to' promising you the world, but a collection of evidence-based techniques and principles that, if implemented, have the power to truly transform your interaction with others. I encourage you to be open-minded, even if you are the most seasoned of communicators, with a view to making small, but steady adjustments to the road to better conversations.

Developing your conversational skills can help you get the most out of your life. In *The Art of Conversation*, I'll show you just how simple it really is.

A note on research: Much research has gone into the way we as humans interact. Please see the end notes in this book for a list of any research I have quoted in the book.

chapter one
What is conversation?

WHAT IS CONVERSATION?

Recently I experienced a classic example of the power of being open to conversation. I'd just finished the first leg of a trip to London via New York. Thirty hours after leaving Sydney, I arrived in New York to be met with the news that my onwards flight had been cancelled due to snowstorms. Joining a long and slow-moving queue to the airline desk, I experienced one of the dilemmas of traveling alone ... should I stay where I was, or explore other potential solutions – which would also mean losing my place in the queue?

Fortunately for me, I struck up a conversation with the couple from New York in front of me. While I was chatting with them they managed to get hold of a reservations phone number and were booked on a flight the following day. My new friends handed the phone over to me and, happily, I also managed to book a seat on a flight leaving the following day.

I wasn't happy to be losing a day in the UK, since I was only heading over for the briefest of catch-ups with my parents, but I was thrilled to know I would be getting out of the airport and, more importantly, could leave the queue after only twenty minutes!

In the end I didn't use the new ticket. As a result of leaving the queue, I was actually able to get on a flight the same day with another airline, losing only half a day of my valuable face-to-face time with my ageing parents – an all-too-rare treat. During the process I had to revisit the original airline to get my ticket released, and saw that the fellow who had been behind me in the queue was only two-thirds of the way through it after more than three hours, and still none the wiser as to when and how he was going to be able to get out of New York.

Worth a conversation? Undoubtedly!

What is successful conversation?

In the hours available to me after that encounter I was reflecting on my good fortune. I began analysing what it was about the conversation I'd had with the strangers in front of me that had allowed them to feel so comfortable that they went on to lend me their phone not once, but twice. It occurred to me that there was no significance in the actual words that were spoken. Instead, it was the words interweaving with what we thought and did that created a positive environment and enabled us to connect.

Traditional communication skills training tends to focus on the significance of listening: 'two ears, and one mouth'. Listening is without a doubt a key component of effective communication, but if you want to be purposeful with your conversations, you need to be consciously aware of what you *say*, *think* and *do*.

Research has shown that the believability of our message is dependent on the consistency between what we are saying, how we are saying it and what we are doing with our hands and faces (our body language). The more consistent we are with these 'say' and 'do' components, the more believable our communication is. The only way we can achieve this consistency is to properly engage our brain in the conversation process so that our *thinking* is also consistent with the message we want to give.

If we are meeting someone for the first time we tend to focus our thoughts on the words we are saying or about to say. Yet ironically, according to communications expert Albert Maharbian,[i] the words themselves only have a marginal influence on how others initially feel about us. The really important thing when it comes to making the right first impression is how we say those words, and what we are physically doing in terms of our body language and facial expressions.

What may be even more surprising is that this need for us to think about how we say our words and what we do physically is still important even when we are involved in information-heavy conversations such as presenting a proposal.

With this kind of communication we again tend to fall into the trap of just thinking about the words we are saying. Don't get me wrong. When you are taking someone through detailed information it is very important that you get the words right. However it is also still very important to get your delivery right in terms of your body language, facial expressions and your tone of voice.

So the key here is: no matter what the conversation, whether you're just chatting or giving an important presentation, as well as *thinking* about your words you also need to be thinking about your *delivery* of those words and *what* you are doing whilst you are talking.

Meet the elements of successful conversation

As you can see, successful conversation is not just about saying and *doing* the right things. It is also about how you are *thinking* – and, most importantly, it's about being *consistent with your thinking*. When your thinking matches what you say and what you do, your conversations work properly for you.

Successful conversations should always be considered as a two-way process between yourself and those you are talking to. The talking should be shared. However that is not to say that everyone has conversations in the same way, nor should they. Life would be very dull if we all spoke in the same way. To be successful in conversation you *always* need to be yourself, while following a few simple rules to enable your conversations to work for you. We'll explore some of the key rules below.

Say

By 'say', I am referring to the actual words we use but also how we say them – our intonation, volume, pitch, pace and emphasis.

As I've already discussed, our words only account for part of our message.[ii] And how we say those words is another important part of the equation. My own experience definitely validates the research – for instance, I've always been interested in how much 'fire in the belly' candidates would demonstrate when interviewing for positions with me. If they can't be passionate about themselves, and show it, why on earth would they be able to get excited about a budgeting system? Their technical knowledge and capability, and the words they use, are of less concern to me than the visual clues – energy, passion, commitment. Although knowledge can be taught, I'm not sure that passion is so easily gained.

> Top Tip: The words you use and how you say them are equally important.

Think

You could be forgiven for thinking that when I discuss 'thinking in conversation' that I'm referring to managing your grey matter. In fact, in many instances, it is actually about *not* thinking rather than thinking! How often do you sabotage the opportunity for a purposeful conversation because of your busy mind? How often have you missed an opportunity to help a child, colleague, or friend simply because you weren't present to their conversation? The trick is to learn how to still your busy mind and be conscious in your thoughts.

Another aspect of thinking in conversation is the limiting beliefs you may have. Do you feel awkward talking with strangers, or talking about yourself with others? Do you question the ability of others and pigeonhole them into a certain category? These beliefs and thoughts can close you off from those you are in conversation with, having the sad consequence of limiting or even sabotaging the potential of the conversation.

In 2007 I made a decision to write a book on the 'art of conversation'. Although I am a professional communicator, this awareness and decision meant that I became even more proactive in engaging in conversations with people I had never met before – and more conscious of being present during those conversations.

One such occasion was on a business trip to Melbourne. On the same day I had two intriguing conversations with the taxi drivers taking me to and from Melbourne airport. What are the chances of having an Iraqi driver both ways on the same day? Interestingly, they represented two sides of the Iraqi regime during Saddam Hussein's presidency. I came away with much greater insights into the challenges and complexities of living through that situation. It also gave me a glimmer of understanding of what it was like for people to survive in such an environment. The lives of the taxi drivers – the lives they'd led before arriving in Melbourne – became much more real to me. And, in turn, I was humbled by the lucky life I have led simply because of when and where I was born. I was also reinvigorated with the feeling of how 'right' it had been to settle in Sydney and to bring up my family in this great country.

Simply opening myself up to conversation with these two men provided me with new insights, mental stimulation, and a sense of gratitude for my own life. All just from a conversation!

> Top Tip: The 'think' part of conversations is about being genuine, being interested, and being present. It's that simple!

Do

For me listening is, in itself, a 'doing' part of conversation. One needs to consciously commit to active listening. It doesn't't happen by chance, but it is more than just 'two ears'. We also need to demonstrate listening through what we 'do' with our eyes, gestures, and body postures. The more our partners in conversation see that we are engaged in the dialogue, the more engaged they will become and the more we will trust each other. When all of these elements are working in together, we can be as 'on purpose' as possible.

Top Tip: Engage in the conversation by actively listening and responding to the other person – show your interest through your body language.

Are you engaging all three?

If you truly want to have successful conversations, then you need to engage all three modes of say, think and do. Conversations, by definition, are held 'between two or more people', and are forums 'in which thoughts, feelings and ideas are expressed, questions are asked and answered, or news and information are exchanged.'[iii] A core value of having a conversation is the willingness to enter into an 'exchange' of dialogue. One of my maxims is 'you need to give to get' – if you give of yourself emotionally, you will receive in return far more than you expected.

What happens if you don't have all three conversational elements of *say, think, do*?

If you currently feel that your conversations are not proving as enriching as they could be, it may just be that one of these key pieces is missing: your *say*, *think* or *do* skills may be under performing. If one of these elements is missing or very weak then you may become a conversational Teller, an Observer or a Confuser.

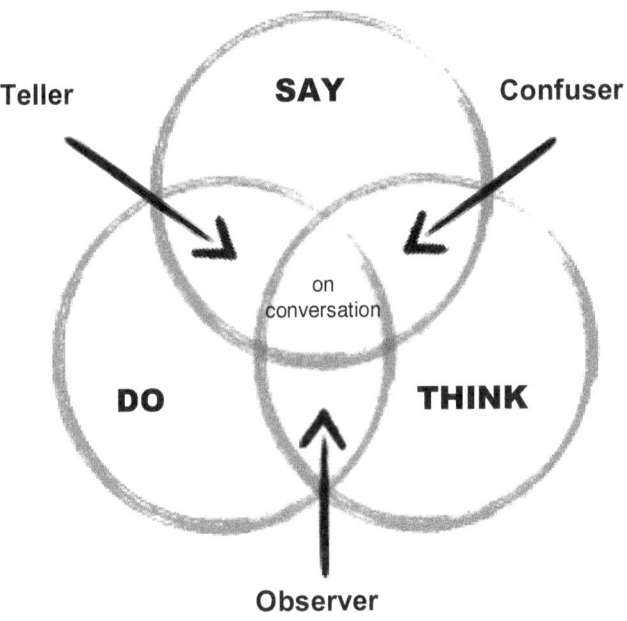

Figure 1. The three types of converters; Teller, Confuser, and Observer, and how these map on to the three components of conversation - Say, Think, Do.

Tellers

If you are strong in the *say* and *do* modes – if you typically do all the talking in the conversation – you may naturally be a 'Teller'. Tellers talk well. They are good at making eye contact, and use their body language well to add to their story.

The problem with Tellers is they don't tend to think about the other people in the conversation. For a Teller, a conversation is more about being heard than about being understood. And although Tellers might be great at delivery, their monopolisation of the conversation can simply become boring.

If this sounds familiar, then it's helpful to recognise that you may polarise people. When this happens, your ability to influence others who don't hold your point of view will be limited.

Allow yourself time to observe a little more and *think* how you can raise the power of your conversation. If you're a Teller, you should try and consider the needs of others more. In order to have a good conversation, the talking needs to be shared, even if you're talking to someone a little on the shy side. If you're with someone who's sitting back in the conversation and not saying anything, make a special effort to include them. Why not try asking them their opinion on the topic you're discussing?

Observers

If you don't perceive yourself as a natural conversationalist, spend more time *thinking* and *doing* than actually *saying* anything, and feel more comfortable being in the audience than participating in the dialogue, then you may well be an Observer. While listening is a wonderful skill – and entirely appropriate during a conversation – the Observer's style ultimately does not help the conversation to progress.

This is not to say you are not interested in the conversation, or even that you are not getting great value out of being part of it. It is just that you are not contributing to the content, the 'say'.

The consequence of this for the Observer is that their passive behaviour in conversations may be interpreted by others as aloof, disinterested or, worse, just plain rude. It might just mean you don't get to borrow the phone, and have an extra three hours in a queue to get what you want.

As an Observer, it's helpful to understand the importance of contributing to the conversation by saying something. You don't have to be an expert or an entertainer – nobody expects that – but it is ideal to participate.

Start off on the easy stuff. For example, make strong acknowledging comments to others, such as:

> 'Oh that's interesting!'
>
> 'I loved the way you ... '
>
> 'Who would have thought it would have turned out that way?'

You can also try asking questions to show you want to hear more and don't forget to make sure your inflection and eye contact demonstrate interest. Questions such as:

> 'So what happened next?'
>
> 'How did you ... ?'
>
> 'Tell me more about ... '

The more you contribute the more your confidence will increase, and gradually, you'll stop being a Observer.

Confusers

Given the power and importance of the visual signals we consciously and unconsciously send out while in conversation, those of you who are not aligning your *do* with what you say and think will be sending out very confusing messages. And as the research has shown any conflict or 'disconnect' between what you say, think and do will reduce the believability and impact of your conversation.

This is incredibly important. If you're saying one thing – even if you're saying it with utter belief – and yet you don't come across as looking as if you believe what you're saying (perhaps you're a nervous public speaker, and your physical actions make you look awkward) then people will lose faith in your words. If you're a Confuser, people will find it hard to develop trust in you.

If your actions are not in alignment with your words then people's BS detectors start twitching big-time. You need to be aware of the subliminal messages you are sending out.

> Top tip: Start observing the body language of others. Get to know the positive and negative body language signals. Be conscious of your own body language, and work on reducing negative signals and employing positive ones in your own communication.

The art of listening

Talking is not the only element of being successful in conversation. Listening to the conversation is equally important, as listening allows the conversation to progress.

Let me give you an example from a networking function I went to recently. These can be challenging at the best of times. Even the most confident of us can find it difficult being thrust into a room with lots of people you don't know, then having to go up and chat to them.

After arriving, I introduced myself to two suited men in their mid-forties who had just started a conversation about wealth creation. One of the men proposed a strategy of property purchase, while the other was more into investing in stocks and shares. They both took turns talking, so they were sharing the talking, yet neither actually appeared to listen to the other.

There was no acknowledgment of each other's standpoint, let alone an appropriate response to what the other had to say. I'd be very surprised if either party benefited or learnt anything from the conversation.

They were happy to spout their views, and even happy to remain silent while the other was talking, but it was clear they weren't listening to each other. The conversation simply didn't progress. It was quite bizarre to witness; it seemed totally futile, not to mention being incredibly boring to listen to, so I moved on.

Both parties must not only be seen to be listening, but must also *actively listen* for the conversation to be successful.

Networking Tips

Good opening questions at a networking function are:

What keeps you busy during the week? (This wording is great as it doesn't discriminate between those in paid employment and those who aren't.)

What are you working on at the moment? (If you can't remember what they do.)

How do you know (the name of the host)?

What happened in the news today? I didn't get a chance to catch it.

Tell me more about your (fishing, golf, exercise class .. etc.).

Only ask one question at a time. If you have asked someone a question listen to their response and maintain eye contact with them for the entire time. As they are responding to your question, make acknowledging statements such as 'yes', 'uh huh', 'I see', 'or 'good'.

Nodding your head and facial expressions also help to show that you are actively listening to them and understand what they are saying.

The two levels of conversation

Have you ever noticed when in conversation with someone that occasionally your voice might quaver or falter over a particular statement? Perhaps the strength in your voice goes, or you suddenly need to clear your throat. These things typically happen when you're making a statement that you are not all that sure about, or if you are trying to conceal something. Similarly, you may find yourself touching your face, scratching your nose or notice that suddenly you've crossed your arms. It's funny, isn't it?

The reason behind these changes in the strength of our voice or our body position is that we actually have our conversations on two levels, a conscious and subconscious level.

The conscious level is where we think about and are aware of what we are doing. Generally in conversations, if we consciously think about anything at all, we are thinking about what we are saying – the words we're using, or what we'll say next.

The subconscious level is where we are not aware of our thoughts. These thoughts help us quickly assess situations and people and produce automatic actions to help us quickly deal with the complexity of everyday living.

A classic example of how the conscious and subconscious work in different ways is driving home from work. Generally, while you drive, you'll find that your mind is busy thinking about the day you've had, what your evening has in store, or what on earth you are going to cook for dinner given the empty shelves in your fridge.

While these thoughts are whizzing around your conscious mind, your subconscious mind instructs your body to drive the car and navigate through the traffic home. Suddenly you are at your front door without even realising it, all through the power of your subconscious mind.

In our conversations we also operate on both these levels. We respond to conversations subconsciously through our body language and our tone of voice and so forth. It is this subconscious level of conversation that can make your voice unexpectedly quaver or cause you to cross your arms, even though *consciously* you might be thinking 'I need to sound relaxed about this' or 'of course I'm not defensive about this'.

For most of the time the two levels of conversation, conscious and subconscious, work well together. What we *say* matches what we are *thinking* and what we are *doing* in terms of our tone of voice, our facial expressions and our body language.

For example, imagine you're telling someone how cold you were on a camping trip. You might find that you're crossing your arms across your body and rubbing them as you would do if you were still on your camping trip. The sentence 'it was so cold' would have the emphasis on the word 'so' and the word cold would be stretched out, 'coooooooold', so that everyone would be clear on your true meaning. It really was *very* cold when you went camping!

The challenge comes with more difficult conversations. For example, you might not be that clear yourself about what you're saying. Or perhaps you don't want the other person to know what you really think, or you simply might not be focused on the conversation.

In any of these cases, although on a conscious level we may try to say the right words, our subconscious has a different view as to what those words should be and how you should be saying them. This is what Freud meant when he coined the term 'parapraxis' – or, what we now know as a 'Freudian slip'. This is where the word you *meant* to say is replaced by the word you were *thinking* of, no matter how inappropriate that might be.[iv] The following example shows just how easy it is to mistakenly include subconscious messages in your conversation.

Trevor runs a small boutique printing company close to the city. His new assistant Jonathan has settled in really well, and Trevor is keen to further develop Jonathan's skills in the business. Trevor is happy with Jonathan, but sometimes finds it hard to understand why Jonathan is so overweight. Trevor himself is a fitness nut and wonders about Jonathan's lifestyle choices.

Jonathan has just completed a long and very complicated job, and Trevor goes over to Jonathan's desk to thank him for all his hard work in getting the job done on time. What Trevor means to say is, 'Thanks Jonathan, you were really fast with that turnaround' ... yet what he finds himself saying is, 'Thanks, Jonathan, you were really fat with that turnaround'.

Trevor is understandably mortified, as is Jonathan.

What happened to Trevor was simple – he was tired, and it was the end of a busy day. He wasn't really concentrating on his conversation. Instead as he was talking to Jonathan he was looking at Jonathan's weight and wondering why such a talented young man would end up being so overweight. And as he was thinking this, his conscious and subconscious conversations simply got mixed up.

So remember – you need to focus and keep your subconscious mind involved in the conversation to avoid mix-ups. Don't allow your thoughts to drift while you're speaking with others!

In another example, Tracey and I were round at friend's place for lunch. Stephen had given James, his youngest son, the task of washing the family car to earn a bit of extra pocket money. James bounded into the house full of enthusiasm after he had washed the car. 'I've finished, Dad', he says with a big grin on his face and suds around his shoes. Everyone smiles. James's enthusiasm is very infectious, and we leave the lunch-table to admire his handiwork.

The car, sitting in the driveway, is still half-covered in suds. There is a dark foam smear that arcs from the front tyre over the drivers' door, and one of the windscreen wipers is at a very odd angle. Stephen's car is his pride and joy; allowing his bouncy eight-year-old to undertake the job in the first place was probably not the best idea.

As he surveyed his beloved car, Stephen's hands shot up automatically to his mouth in a desperate attempt to stop himself from saying what a dreadful job he thought James had done. He quickly recovered, and you could see his brain was now consciously engaged as he pulled his hands down away from his face. He consciously knew he should be positive. 'Well, haven't you been busy,' he said. 'We can certainly see you've been hard at work soaping the car, that's not a bad job James'.

The words were not great, but passable given the circumstances. Where Stephen fell down was in the way he'd delivered the words. As he spoke he'd moved his arms across his chest and a hand snuck up towards his mouth again. His voice was shakier than usual, and his initial smile had quickly disappeared. And not only that, but he had emphasised the word 'bad' – because that is what he really thought of the job. It *was* a bad job and that is probably why he chose to use that word. Juggling his disappointment over the job James had done and his wish to praise his son, Stephen had delivered the sentence 'that's not a bad job, James' with an implied meaning: it's not a *good* job, either.

Now don't panic – no one can get it right all the time, and if they could, they wouldn't be human. Simply being aware of some of the classic pitfalls in our conversations, and seeing how our statements can be so misunderstood, is really powerful in itself.

chapter two
Say

Say

Words are a powerful tool, and it's just as easy to use them well as it is to use them badly, or to ill effect. Following are some simple rules about words.

No

No is an interesting word. I am sure it was one of the first words my children learnt, and as young children they used it over and over again. At one point I began to question where they had learnt this favourite word of theirs from. Hmmm ... I listened to myself on a family outing to the zoo. 'No, you can't have a photo taken with a koala'; 'No you can't have an ice cream'; 'No, I won't be buying you a toy monkey'.

What I eventually worked out was that the word 'no' has an amazing boomerang effect. That is, the more you say it, the more it bounces back at you – and the less impact it has.

Using 'no' on adults produces a similar response to that of my children. Adults don't like being told 'no' either, and will quickly start responding negatively if they hear the word directed at them too often.

The trick with 'no' is to reduce the amount of times you actually use the word. This does two things. First, it reduces the build-up of negative responses to what you have to say. Second, it gives 'no' far greater impact when you do actually say it.

One of the best ways to avoid using the word no is to say yes instead. Let's have a look at a couple of examples.

You've been asked to take on another task at work that you really don't feel you have the time to do. Try wording it like this:

'Yes, I would be happy to do that project for you. I have two projects currently on the go, and they will take me three weeks to complete. So I could start your project after that.' (In other words you've said 'no, I can't do it now'.)

Your friend has asked you to help her move again.

'I would love to help you move, but I am having physio on my back at the moment and am not allowed to lift anything. Perhaps I could pop in later in the week to help celebrate your move instead?' (In other words, 'no, I can't help you move'.)

> Top Tip: Reduce your 'no's to reduce negative responses coming back and to give your occasional 'no's real impact.

Don't

Another word with negative connotations is don't. Statements such as 'don't do this' and 'don't do that' become very grating. You often see signs in office kitchens where someone has clearly had enough of the mess:

'Don't leave dirty dishes in the sink!'

'Don't put wet tea towels on the bench!'

'Don't put the dishwasher on cycle two!'

'Don't leave the fridge door open!'

There is something about 'don't' that brings out the rebellious side of people. The more "don't's" there are, the more likely someone is to leave a dirty teaspoon in the sink while no one is looking. Additionally, the word 'don't' seems to create selective blindness, where strangely, nobody sees the 'don't' sign and just sees the command to put the dishwasher on cycle two. A good example of this is what we choose to say to our young children at night when we are trying to help them combat bed wetting. We put them in nappies, have a rubber sheet on the bed and spend the last few moments asking them not to wet the bed tonight. "Don't wet the bed" simply results in their last thought before going to sleep being about wetting the bed. Guess what, they wet the bed.

An alternative is to focus on 'What would you like to do first thing in the morning when you wake up with a dry bed and we can get straight into the day?

Top Tip: Rather than use 'don't', use 'do'. Tell people what you want them to do and tell them why they should do it rather than telling them what you don't want them to do, or how they shouldn't do it.

The same is true with verbal instructions. Parents shout to stop children running around a swimming pool with the instruction 'Don't run!' Pools are noisy places. It's more than likely that the kids won't clearly hear or be sure about the first word; at that point they are still identifying their parents' voices over the noise of others. And what happens is that they tune in clearly for the second word, 'RUN!'

'Sally, how about walking? That way you won't slip.'

'Would you please use cycle three for the dishwasher to avoid jamming the machine.'

'Please hang the tea towels on the hooks so they dry ready for their next use.'

Top Tip: Too many instructions, no matter how well worded they might be, can be seen as condescending. In fact, too many instructions will bring out the rebellious streak in just about anyone. So pick the key things you want to address and leave the less important things for another time.

Would and could

If you really want action from others, try using 'would' instead of 'could'. Compare these two statements:

'Would you put the bins out?'

'Could you/can you put the bins out?'

'Would you put the bins out?' is a polite request for action. The person you are asking will feel they have choice in the matter.

They're unlikely to feel that they are being told what to do, and more often than not, they'll happily carry out your request!

'Could you/can you put the bins out?' is more an assessment of capability than a request. Typically it generates a response of, 'Yes I can'; however, it doesn't generate action. The person responding to your question isn't really being difficult – they have simply answered your question. You have just asked them the wrong question!

Next time, remember to use would instead of could, and see the difference a word makes.

Always and never

'Always' and 'never' are two words that will regularly prompt others – especially your nearest and dearest – to correct your statement. My best advice is to bin these words altogether. For example, statements such as:

'I always buy organic fruit and veg!' will have your husband recalling the time you bought tomatoes from the expensive non-organic corner shop.

'I never forget our anniversary' will be swiftly corrected by your partner reminding you how on your first anniversary you had booked to go skiing with the lads.

To avoid being corrected, avoid using 'always' and 'never'. Words such as 'regularly' and 'rarely' are far more likely to be left alone and not contradicted.

But and however

'But' and 'however' are interesting linking words people use to join two statements together. Be aware that the use of these linking words actually changes the implied meaning of the sentence. For example:

'Your dress looks lovely but wouldn't you rather wear that red skirt? It'll be warmer.' (The implied meaning that the other person hears is: that dress doesn't look as good as the red skirt – or maybe it doesn't look lovely at all.)

'You're doing well, however you need to tighten up your project time-lines.' (The implied meaning the other person hears is: I am in trouble for running late with my projects.)

To avoid your message being misunderstood simply drop 'but' and 'however' and keep the sentences separate.

'Your dress looks lovely.' (Here, add a pause for the first sentence to sink in.) 'Are you going to be warm enough in that?'

'You're doing well with these projects, we've very happy with your work.' (Again, add a pause for the first sentence's meaning to sink in.) 'Let's have a look at the time-lines and see if it's possible to tighten them up any further.'

Top Tip: Drop 'but' and 'however' from your vocabulary to avoid misunderstandings.

Stop the jargon and keep people interested

When you are talking to anyone who is not a direct colleague, ensure you steer clear of office jargon. Work jargon and highbrow intellectual statements are fine for those in the know, but for those not in the know they can be very hard to understand.

Using non-inclusive language can make people feel as though they are being intentionally excluded from the conversation. It is rare that people will ask you what something means, because they don't want to appear stupid. Instead they will simply stop listening – and if no one is listening, you are not in conversation.

It is not just what you say ... it's what you choose to emphasise

We have seen how our choice of words can impact on how our conversations progress. What is often underestimated, though, is that how we deliver these words can greatly affect the meaning and impact of our statement.

Our voice is an amazing communication tool, and we have the power to use it to great effect. We can speak louder to gain attention or reduce the volume to add impact or intrigue, drawing the crowd in. We can speed up the pace to energise the group or slow down our pace to help others to gain greater understanding.

Also, simply changing the emphasis in a sentence can totally change the implied meaning. For example, the sentence 'We didn't steal your wallet' can be read in various ways. First, try emphasising the word 'we'. Then read the sentence again emphasising the word 'didn't'; next, read it again, emphasising 'steal', and so forth. See the table opposite for a full explanation.

"We didn't steal your wallet"	
Placing emphasis on ...	Implied meaning
'we'	Someone else did
'didn't'	We didn't steal your wallet
'steal'	Your wife gave it to us
'your'	It was someone else's wallet
'wallet'	We stole something else

People often don't realise how important delivery is – the way you say the things you say. Take the example of my partner, who has a pretty loud voice. So loud, in fact, that the whole family can hear her from anywhere in the house. Yet if her message is really important she will often talk really softly, and she slows down her delivery so we don't miss a thing. It's quite spooky the impact her soft, slow voice has on us.

The other day while dinner was cooking, she was telling our children the importance of waiting for the 'green man' before crossing the road, and I found myself drawn to the conversation in the kitchen. It was only just audible, so I had to go closer to hear.

There was something about the way she was telling it that made me want to listen!

She found it highly amusing that I listened so intently to the entire story. I told her that she shouldn't be surprised. If you pay good attention to your delivery you should be able to expect that people will stop and listen to you – because you're saying things in a way that is intended to interest people.

> Top Tip: Pause after important sentences so that others have time to consider what you have to say. Don't rush it!

In order for you to get the most from your voice, consider the following.

- Think about your normal speaking voice. Are you naturally loud, soft, fast, or slow in your everyday speech?
- How could you vary your tone to add impact to your words?
- When would it be appropriate to slow down, speed up, talk loudly or softly?
- Who are you talking to? How well can they hear you? Are there distracting noises in the background?
- What is the situation? Is this social chit-chat or are you chairing a meeting?

- How does the person you're talking to normally talk? If they are fast talkers, are they going to get bored if you talk slowly, or vice versa?

- How do you want to come across, e.g. relaxed, or in control?

- Which words should you give the greatest emphasis to?

> Top Tip: Don't be afraid to practice and vary your delivery. Think of how actors in movies are directed to articulate their lines to keep their audience engaged. That's no different to you keeping your audience engaged in your conversation – so work at it, and do it with flair!

Stress the similarities and minimise the differences

Most people react positively to others who are either in agreement with them or have similar opinions or views. So when you are trying to build rapport with someone new, the art of good conversation is to find areas of similarity and agreement, and to place focus on those while avoiding dwelling on areas of disagreement or difference. Look for visual clues, such as the paper the other person reads, where they buy their coffee, the clothes they wear or the car they drive. These will all give you a starting point in stressing the similarities. Alternatively, find out what books they like to read, what plays or films they have seen recently, or what sport they follow or participate in. Then follow up the conversation by stressing the enjoyment you get from reading, watching or playing similar things.[v]

Be nice

Most people like others who like them. Simple, really! To help your conversation skills develop, aim to always be nice to those you talk to.[vi]

When you first run into someone or begin a meeting, be enthusiastic about seeing them. Be genuine, and express the sentiment, 'It's really lovely to see you' with your voice, your facial expressions and your body language. When you first see someone, smile and make your whole face light up with that smile – including your eyes. People aren't easily fooled – if you're not being genuine, others can generally tell. Ask them how they are and actively listen to their response.

Being nice is a great basic foundation for any interaction. But I'll let you in on a secret: people especially like verbal flattery. They even prefer someone saying something nice about them than someone actually doing them a favour.[vii] Not only does flattery make people like you more, studies have shown that flattery can help you get better pay increases and promotions, so it is well worth the effort to pay people compliments.[viii] When you next bump into someone, as well as telling them how great it is to see them, tell them how good they look, or what great work they have done, or how helpful they were. The more specific the flattery, the more believable it is, and the more they will love hearing it.

This is not to say that you should flatter purely with the aim of bettering your lot. Not at all! But it's possible to offer genuine flattery to everyone, no matter what your personal feelings about them. For example, you may have a colleague you don't always see eye-to-eye with – but that shouldn't stop you commenting on a nice new tie he's wearing. As always, it is about being authentic in your conversation.

Top Tip: Avoid statements that imply something negative about others.

'Have you had your hair cut?'

Think about it ... what are you trying to say here? Does their hair look great or terrible? If it looks lovely then tell them, but if it looks terrible, don't mention it and talk about something else.

'So when's the baby due?'

If you haven't been told a woman is pregnant never assume that she might be. It could just be a very unflattering top that makes her look pregnant – and you can rest assured she won't thank you for the comment.

Use questions to help your conversation progress

Questions are a great tool for conversations. Effective questioning helps:

- Build rapport in the initial stages of a conversation
- Get a conversation going
- Keep a conversation on track
- Involve others
- Stop others from monopolising the conversation.

Use open questions, that is, questions that cannot be answered by 'yes' or 'no'. Questions that begin with the following words invite ideas and discussion, and are perfect for helping the conversation progress:

- 'How'
- 'What'
- 'Where'
- 'When'
- 'Which'
- 'Tell me about'
- 'Who'.

Avoid 'Why?' as a question, and use 'Tell me about' instead to open people up in discussion. It's best to avoid it because 'why' has two possible interpretations. People use it either for asking a purpose or a reason. When you are asking someone about their purpose you are asking about their intent; you are seeking to understand. On the other hand, when you are asking someone for their reason for something, you are asking for justification, and the question can be interpreted as being demanding. Typically people will interpret 'why' as if you are demanding a justification. Hence, they may become defensive and give you a snappy response.

Chapter three
Think

THINK

The 'think' part of successful conversations is all about being aware. You need to be aware of the power of being open to and present in each conversation you have. You also need to be aware of your own limiting beliefs so that you can counteract or change them. The more aware you are, the more you'll find yourself benefiting from and enjoying your conversations.

The positive side of the 'think' part of conversations is how much you can learn from interactions with people, and how much you can impart when talking to them. These benefits come from a successful conversation where you have been mentally engaged.

The negative side of the coin, however is when you are busy thinking ... but not about the conversation at hand. This competing thought-process or internal conversation can be very distracting and can really impact on the success of your conversation.

One of the typical internal conversations we have is with what we term our *monkey*. This is a term we use with our clients to describe the inner voice we all have. We find that by naming it your 'monkey' – making it at once vaguely silly, and external to you – it becomes easier for you to be aware of it and to control it.

Your monkey speaks a universal language, and everyone has their own monkey. It speaks all the languages of the world and will always communicate to you in your native tongue. You would imagine, being so linguistically competent, that a speaking monkey would be fascinating to listen to, but sadly it spends most of the time repeating itself. You'll also notice that it generally hasn't got anything nice to say.

How can I recognise monkey-chatter?

Monkey-chatter is quite easy to recognise, It usually opens with the phrase, 'but you can't' or something equally negative. The theme is always the same (no matter how linguistically eloquent it is) and it's 'LET'S GET OUT OF HERE!'

Your monkey is particularly noisy when you are in new or stressful exchanges, in or out of work. Although the monkey's purpose is to 'protect' you from embarrassing situations, it is often the monkey's negative commentary that can lead you into the same embarrassing situations it was trying to protect you from.

A client I was coaching, Daniel, revealed how infuriating his monkey-chatter could be in one of his sessions.

Daniel had met his old school friend Peter in the local pub. He was very comfortable with this conversation as he has known Peter for years. His monkey saw no need to 'protect' Daniel, and 'slept' through the conversation. Then Angela, Peter's cousin, appeared. Daniel had always thought Angela was a very attractive woman and here was an opportunity for Daniel to ask Angela out for dinner. The monkey stirred.

Daniel's first couple of sentences engaging with Angela went well (his monkey was still stretching and hadn't quite got to grips with the situation), but it didn't take long before the monkey was wide awake and started chatting to Daniel. The monkey said things like:

'She is far too good looking for you.'

'Just look at your big stomach!'

'Ha, your neck is starting to redden, you're embarrassed.'

'I'd quit now before you say anything stupid.'

'See, that was a stupid thing to say!'

... and so on. This was of course very distracting for Daniel and gradually he started to listen more to his monkey than to Angela. Sure enough, as the monkey had predicted, the conversation went downhill.

And what happened? Angela interpreted Daniel's apparent distractedness and increasing awkwardness as a lack of interest in her. She returned to her group of friends and left Daniel feeling just as stupid as his monkey predicted he would.

Managing your monkey

1. Be aware of and accept that you have a monkey.
2. Recognise your monkey's statements as *false* statements.
3. Don't fight the monkey; just notice it for what it is. In time it will calm down. The more attention you pay it, the more power it has over you.
4. Stay focused on the external conversation. If you get distracted in a conversation just admit it. Why not say, 'I'm really sorry but I was completely distracted for a moment. Tell me more about ... '
5. Always be prepared for a return visit from your monkey.

Now that you've met your monkey, you are in a position to be more aware of it and to pay it less attention. This will allow you to move on to the next step, which is to be more present in your conversations.

Be present

Having a good conversation with someone is about being able to connect with them, exploring and seeking to understand their thoughts and experiences. You're aiming to find out what they think and how they feel.

A good conversationalist needs clear head-space so they can listen properly to what the other person says, as well as being able to formulate appropriate responses. Clear head-space means you need to be mentally present in your conversation as well as physically present.

Sometimes with our busy lives it can be hard enough just physically getting to our meeting or social engagement on time. And after a long, hard day, it can be all too easy to let our minds wander to the huge list of things we have still to do, or back to something during the day that didn't go quite as planned. When we allow our thoughts to wander, we stop being mentally present and we stop listening properly. We have gone back into our world – not the world of the person we're talking to – and the conversation connection is lost.

Three-step plan to stay present in your conversations

1. Consider whether now is the time for that conversation. If you're likely to be preoccupied because you haven't finished an important presentation, it might be better to focus on that first. Rain-check the meeting or social event for another day when you can be fully present and give others the full attention they deserve.

2. If now is the time for that conversation, when you walk into the room, visualise leaving all your 'thought baggage' of past events and future things by the door. They will be nice and safe there. 'Leaving your thoughts at the door' allows you to fully focus on the conversation at hand. Rest assured when you leave the room all your thoughts will return to you.

3. When you are in conversation and a distracting thought comes to mind, you have two choices. Either visualise your thought in a bubble and mentally blow it away, or choose not to engage with the thought and simply jot down a reminder. This way you can focus on the conversation and not on trying to remember the thought.

Respect others - and yourself

When in a conversation with someone, talk to them the way you would like to be spoken to. Respect them for who they are and assume they have something valid to say. If you don't respect them, your true feelings are likely to become apparent through your subconscious body language, your voice and facial expressions.

It's equally important to respect yourself in conversation. Acknowledge that you too have something valid to say so that you hold your head up high and deliver your messages clearly. Don't put yourself or your opinions down!

Understand that everyone has a right to an opinion. Your opinions and those of others are equally valid – even if you violently disagree with theirs, or if theirs turn out to be right … which can be hard to take!

We had some friends visit us from New Zealand. Mum, Dad and their older kids arrived and it was wonderful to hear the different generations in conversation. One evening we had just finished dinner and settled down to a glass of wine when the topic of music arose. It was a classic conversation. The younger members of the family were talking about various bands they knew, how great they were and what musical talent was around.

'What rubbish' said their mother, who is very musically talented. 'What do you know about music?' She then proceeded to tell them in no uncertain terms that they didn't know what they were talking about and that they were wrong.

At this point I have to confess that I saw where this conversation was headed and chose to 'duck out' by sliding further down in my chair and carefully examining the sediment in the bottom of my glass. The point here is that the views of the younger family members were not respected and as a result, the conversation turned ugly quickly.

What should have happened?

To turn the conversation around, Mum could instead have asked questions along the lines of: What is musical talent? Where did those musicians get their inspiration from? Would you still be able to hear talent in those that play a style of music that doesn't appeal to you? By asking these questions, she'd be endeavouring to understand the kids' views, and potentially even finding common ground with them.

Respecting someone and their viewpoint is about trying to understand who that person is, where they are coming from and why they might say the things they say. You don't have to agree with them. When you start to look at the person holistically rather than judging them purely on their statements, you will find it easier to converse with and understand those that are different. It will be less taxing and less frustrating, and easier to find common ground

> *The true spirit of conversation consists in building on another man's observations, not overturning them.*
> *– Robert Bulwer-Lytton (1803–1873)*

Have balance with those you talk to

Picture some old-fashioned scales that have the same weight on either side. The scales need to be level and balanced in order to be effective. This is how you should view yourself and your conversational partner. You should both be balanced and talk to each other on the same level. If, for example, you are talking to your employees and you feel that they are 'below' you, then you will probably come across as condescending and your views will be ignored. Conversely if you are talking to your CEO and your view is that he is 'above' you, you will probably get tongue-tied and say very little, which will get in the way of your view coming across properly.

> Top Tip: Aim to be balanced and level in your conversations and talk to all with the same respect and balance you would have with a good friend.

When to speak and when not to speak

Very broadly, people tend to fall into one of two categories of personality, introverts or extroverts. These personality traits heavily impact on whether we say too much or too little.

Extroverts like the company of others and happily engage in conversation with them.[ix] Extroverts are also more likely to speak before they think. For this reason, their challenge is obvious: words can come streaming out of their mouths before they have thought carefully about what should be said or which words should have been used. Extroverts leaving a social function are more likely to think 'I wish I hadn't said that!'

Introverts prefer to avoid the company of others and typically shy away from large social gatherings.[x] Introverts are more likely to think before they speak, and on paper that sounds good. In reality what happens is introverts take too long thinking about what they are going to say and the conversation has well and truly moved on before they get round to saying anything. On leaving a social function introverts are more likely to think, 'I wish I had said ... '

> *'The real art of conversation is not only to say the right thing at the right place but to leave unsaid the wrong thing at the tempting moment.'*
> – Dorothy Neville, author of Under Five Reigns (1910)

Are you are an extrovert or an introvert? The following section suggests tips for both personality types in conversation.

When you say too much

I am sure we have all done it: glibly said something, and then wished we could press the rewind button because it didn't come out as planned. Or perhaps this wasn't the best time to say those things. Either way there is a great desire to erase the statement from the minds of those present.

Last year I had one of those moments. A good friend of ours came over for dinner. She was sporting a fabulous short haircut that looked really striking. I complimented her on how great she looked and how much the cut added to her looks (all good so far). I then went on to say how it was about time she had her very long hair cut, as it was quite ageing. It was then she revealed she was wearing a wig and the long hair was still very much intact! Ahh, if only I had a rewind button. Thankfully I did a reasonable job of re-emphasising how great it was to see her looking so young and refreshed. Then I moved the conversation swiftly on to her lovely children which seemed to get me out of the mess my need to talk too much had got me into.

Conversation tips for extroverts:

- Avoid hogging the conversation. Ensure you let others speak.

- Focus on listening fully to what the other person is saying rather than working out what you are going to say next.

- Ask questions to involve others in the conversation, and remember to listen to their response, and look at them while they're responding.

- When you are asked a 'tricky' question, take a breath and allow yourself to pause for a second. It doesn't need to be long, just enough time for you to think before your speak.

- If you are on a roll with a conversation, consider the fact that less is more and maybe it is time to stop!

> *'It is alright to hold a conversation but you should let go of it now and then.'*
> *– Richard Armour (1906–1989), poet*

When you say too little

The other challenge is when you don't speak up and you leave a conversation feeling really frustrated and wishing you had said something.

Does this sound familiar? A friend, we'll call her "Anne", (an extrovert), recently caught up with her very dear friend "Jo" (an introvert). Having already seen each other for dinner that week, Anne called Jo up and suggested it might be fun going to a movie instead. They trotted along to see the action movie The Bourne Ultimatum. As they left the cinema Anne, who was pumped and very chatty after thoroughly enjoying this fast-paced movie, asked Jo what she thought of it.

Jo paused, as introverts do, and then confessed to falling asleep in the movie. Anne was stunned. It turned out Jo was actually very tired that day; she had been working hard all week. It also transpired that Jo didn't actually like action movies and that really surprised Anne. When I next saw Anne, she was rather deflated.

'I feel really guilty,' she said. 'In my enthusiastic way I dragged Jo along to a movie she knew she would hate. Why didn't she say something?' And there's the point. If Jo had spoken up in the beginning she might have had a far more enjoyable evening over a quiet dinner or watching a movie more to her taste – and Anne could have seen the action movie another time.

Conversation tips for introverts:

- If something doesn't work for you, or you don't agree, you need to voice your opinion. Silence will be taken as acceptance.

- Smile more! It is a great opener to conversations and encourages others to talk to you.

- Expand on your yes or no responses to questions asked of you. Fuller responses give others more information to work on and help the conversation to progress.

- If you have something to add to a conversation, SAY IT.

- If you can't think of anything to add then ask a question.

It's not about you

A talented conversationalist recognises that a good conversation isn't just about themselves. Rather, it is about involving others, and listening to what others have to say. Our son has a friend at school whose father has had a very successful public career. He has been the CEO of several large organisations and now is a thriving author. You know he is full of ideas and strong opinions, yet every time we meet the first thing he does is to ask us questions about our day, the school soccer, our son and so forth, and then he listens intently to our answers as though we are the only ones in the room. It makes you feel great, the conversation starts very well, and of course you are then more than happy to listen to what he has to say too.

Seven tips for sharing conversation

1. Ask questions to include others in the conversation.
2. Listen and focus on what the other person is saying.
3. Stop thinking about similar stories you have to tell. This moment isn't about you, it is about the other person.
4. Make acknowledging comments about things the other person says, such as 'That must have been really hard for you', 'Oh wow', 'That's very interesting', 'Really', 'Uh huh' – these show that you are listening, interested and engaged.
5. Find out more from them by asking: 'Tell me more', 'How did you find ...?' 'What happened next ...?'
6. Resist jumping in. Let them finish their story.
7. Maintain strong eye contact with them and avoid being distracted.

> Top Tip: Sometimes the best thing you can do to contribute to a conversation is shut up!

How can I help you?

Okay. Let's be honest here – who has gone to a function with a hidden agenda? I know I have. I have turned up to events because I thought I might get new business from someone I meet. Of course, it is not exclusive to the business world either. You might turn up at a school function hoping to find another parent who you can car-pool with, or perhaps you arrive at an acquaintance's party hoping to meet someone new.

Don't misunderstand me; there is absolutely nothing wrong in striving to get more business, sorting out car-pools or finding a partner. Often, though, the easiest way to get others to help you is to help them first.

When you enter a function with the question, 'Who can help me?' you give out subconscious signals that you are self-focused. Naturally, these signals are not very appealing to others. Without realising it, you may find yourself not listening properly or cutting others off because you don't perceive they can be of help to you. You potentially can come across as distracted or, even worse, arrogant.

By changing your approach to 'How can I help you?', it not only makes you far more appealing to have a conversation with, it also encourages others to open up and reveal possible opportunities for helping each other. When you're blinkered by your own agenda, it's much harder to see these opportunities, or to get others to open up with their own suggestions.

The great news is that you don't have to offer to help in a big way. Maybe you can be a sounding-board for someone else's new idea, maybe you have a contact that would help them, or maybe you know of a service they could use that might make their life easier.

As I write this it takes me back to a time when my partner and I were endeavouring to help Claire, a friend of ours, meet a new man. We were at a mutual friend's party and my partner was out and about surveying the scene. She came across a lovely guy, David, and managed to engineer a conversation between him and Claire. Unfortunately Claire stopped participating in the conversation within minutes and David understandably made a polite excuse and escaped to the bar. My partner was furious. 'What was up with you then?' she asked Claire, who is normally very chatty.

'He wasn't my type!' was Claire's response.

'I know he wasn't your type, he happens to be a lovely married man,' my partner responded. 'He also happens to have several single friends who sounded great and I had offered to help organise a joint dinner party where we could all catch up.

'Oh,' said Claire.

> Top Tip: When meeting others, think: How can I help you? Keep an open mind to the conversation. Think of it as adding value not obligation, and give freely – which in turn will open the door for others to help you.

chapter four
Do

Do

When someone stops and listens attentively to you, doesn't it makes you feel great? It makes you feel appreciated and understood. Conversely, isn't it frustrating when people don't listen to you? Sometimes it can even be really hurtful.

Listening to others is one of the biggest compliments we can give. It is a vital skill to help a conversation be successful ... so why is it that so many of us are so bad at doing it?

Once more, it comes down to personality type, and different methods of dealing with conversation. The following section explores some of the reasons we fail to listen properly through the various different 'types' of listeners. You might recognise yourself here.

Busy Bee listeners

Busy Bees have busy minds and are often preoccupied with thinking about numerous things at once. Their mind flits between things they should do, things they shouldn't do, their daily 'to do' lists, past conversations and future possibilities. Busy Bees with busy thoughts struggle to stay focused on one thing. Your conversation competes with the Busy Bee's internal conversations, as in the example below.

Sarah was getting frustrated with her partner Daniel. She kept on trying to raise the issue of who was responsible for the various household chores. However every time she raised the issue, Daniel quickly moved the conversation onto another track, such as household budgets or potential property investments. Clearly Daniel's mind is occupied with financial issues and it is those thoughts that spring to the forefront when the word household is raised.

Sarah was understandably frustrated and felt Daniel wasn't listening to her. It wasn't that Daniel didn't want to listen or that he was actively avoiding his share of housework – he simply allowed his Busy Bee mind to hijack the conversation.

If you know a Busy Bee listener:

Choose your time carefully with Busy Bees. If you really want them to listen to you, 'now' may not be the best time. Try asking them when would be good to catch up. If you need to talk to them immediately but want their full attention, say: 'I need to talk to you about X. It won't take more than five minutes and I would really appreciate you listening.'

If they break eye contact, start fiddling with something else or just appear to stop focusing on what you are saying, stop dead in the middle of what you are saying. They will realise quickly that something is amiss because there is complete silence. They will look back to you quizzically. At this point you don't really need to say anything – just smile in appreciation of their attention and resume the conversation.

Alternatively, if they look like they have gone off into their busy mind once again, just ask them a question such as:

'What would you do in this situation?'

'Which project do you think I should tackle first?'

'How would you respond to this?'

'Who would you involve?'

In order to answer a question like this you have had to have been listening. The questions will prompt them to pay attention.

When Busy Bees do make the effort to listen to you, make sure you thank them for doing so.

Puppy dog listeners

Puppy Dog listeners are great to start off with. They will sit down and look at you in eager anticipation of what you have to say. They are looking for someone to entertain them, someone to pay them attention. The challenge for Puppy Dog listeners is they can't sit still for long and will quickly get distracted by something else mid-conversation. You haven't even started discussing the important stuff and they have raced outside to put the bins out, felt the need to dust the television or just checked to see if someone has sent them an email. You look at them in amazement and they sheepishly return to you, sit back down again, often most apologetically. You start to explain your situation once more, they look at you – trying so very hard to sit still – and then, thank goodness, the phone rings and they are up once again out of their seat chasing another distraction.

If you know a Puppy Dog listener:

Choose your location for your discussion carefully. It should be well away from distractions. Meeting rooms and coffee shops are good (although in coffee shops always make sure they have their back to the door so they are less distracted by the comings and goings of others).

Keep what you have to say short and get to the point quickly. Try and make it as relevant to them as you can. Tell them up front why they should listen to you, so they know what's in it for them. This helps them stay focused. If they have listened well and have not been distracted, thank them for listening, telling them how much you appreciate it.

Crocodile listeners

Crocodiles listeners are prone to making snap decisions, usually quite early on in your discussion. From the moment you start talking they are assessing whether or not they are going to agree with you and they will be looking for evidence, facts and figures to support their decision.

A comment like 'Let's go away for the weekend' will receive this sort of response from a Crocodile listener: 'Well, where were you thinking? When? Why? What will we do with the dog?'

They want to quickly delve into the detail when all you really wanted was a general agreement to go away. Without thinking, you are caught trying to answer some of these questions that you haven't necessarily thought through. When this happens, you might start listing possible locations or dates off the top of your head, and before you know it the Crocodile makes a snap assessment. 'No I can't go that weekend, it's my mother's birthday.' And that's it. They've closed their ears. The conversation is effectively over, and you are left wondering: how did that happen!?

If you know a Crocodile listener:

Getting Crocodiles to listen is all about how you set up the conversation at the very beginning. You need to raise the concerns or issues they have right up front. Acknowledge their point of view or what you perceive to be their point of view. If you are talking about a weekend away, tell them you know they have a busy diary and there are lots of functions coming up. At this stage, all you would like to do is see if you can put a possible date in the diary and then you can look at where you want to go further down the track.

If it is a more contentious issue, ask them if they would be able to listen openly to your point of view. If during your conversation you feel they have stopped listening, ask them what their thoughts are. Make sure you listen to their thoughts and acknowledge their point of view. Of course, acknowledging someone else's viewpoint doesn't mean you have to agree with it!

Once you have acknowledged their point of view, go back to yours with a linking comment such as 'Yes, I can see where you are coming from, where I am coming from is ... ' Always keep your voice calm and maintain good eye contact with them.

At the end of the conversation, if they have been able to be open to your comments, thank them for their openness.

Bragger listeners

Braggers can give the illusion they are listening when you are telling your story. They will remain seated and probably maintain eye contact. But don't be fooled. While you are regaling them with the bizarre incident you witnessed on the train yesterday they are busily thinking of an even 'better' story, probably based in darkest Africa and involving ferocious lions and a bicycle!

When you pause to take breath the Bragger will invariably jump in with their bigger and better story. They rarely acknowledge your story – which is not surprising because they didn't really listen to it.

If you know a Bragger listener:

To stop a Bragger in their tracks, the first step is to stop them from formulating a 'better' story. To do this you need to keep them involved in your story. Again, asking questions is a good starting point. Ask closed questions such as :

'Do you ...?'

'Would you ...?'

'Is it ...?'

'Have you ...?'

Asking questions during your storytelling signals to the Bragger that they need to listen to you properly so that they'll know what the question is about.

Closed questions are the perfect questions to ask a Bragger, as they only require a yes/no response which avoids allowing the Bragger to talk for too long.

If you have used this technique to tell your great story, but the Bragger fails to acknowledge it and begins to tell their 'better' story, then it is time for step two.

If there is just the two of you, interrupt them and tell them how you feel. Note that you should never give negative feedback to anyone in front of others. Try saying something like:

'Stewart, you made no comment to my story. I didn't sense that you were really listening to me, which I find really hurtful.' Or:

'Stewart, I know you have lived a vivid life and you have lots of great stories, I feel sometimes that you tell one of your great stories simply to upstage mine and it makes me feel very deflated when that happens.'

Most Braggers at this point will throw their apologies at you, telling you of course they were listening and it certainly wasn't their intention to upstage you. Whether it was or wasn't their intention, accept their apology graciously. You have made your point.

If you are in a group it would be inappropriate to give the Bragger negative feedback. In this case, you can simply avoid rewarding them for their one-upmanship by breaking your eye contact with them and drawing your body away from them. They may well ask you later what the problem was and you can give them your feedback then.

Now we have explored the various kinds of flawed listeners and looked at how they should best be handled, let's have a look at my ten tips to help you improve your listening.

Ten tips to help you improve your listening skills

1. Look at the person talking and maintain eye contact, so you can 'hear' with your eyes as well as your ears.

2. Stop your busy mind, now is not the time.

3. Be in their world not yours; remember it's not all about you.

4. Don't interrupt or talk over them; let them finish their story.

5. Be open to what they have to say and suspend judgement.

6. Avoid selective listening. It's not just about what you *want* to hear.

7. Make acknowledging statements during their conversation such as 'I see', 'Uh huh', and appropriate nods and facial gestures to show your understanding.

8. Remove distractions, turn off the television, and switch off the computer or telephone when you're talking with others.

9. Be physically still and avoid fidgeting.

10. Never be too busy to listen.

Stephan Covey, who wrote the book *7 Habits of Highly Effective People,* talks about the importance of empathic listening. He explains the trap most of us fall into when in conversation is, we seek to be understood rather than seeking to understand the person we are in conversation with. He goes on to explain empathic listening is about seeing the world from their view point and to understand the feelings of the person you are talking to. So according to Covey not only do you need to 'listen' with your eyes and ears you also need to listen with your heart so you can hear the emotional messages being conveyed.

Listening is a really difficult thing to do effectively, especially with our busy lives and busy minds. A famous study showed that, on average, GPs interrupt their patients' opening statement after only eighteen seconds! What is also surprising is that patients only needed approximately two and a half minutes to tell the GP the full reason for their consultation.[xi] This is a little alarming when you consider that GPs are people you'd really like to be listening to you fully! So learn from their mistakes and always remember to listen fully to others so you get the whole picture.

Of course some people are easier to listen to than others. Make sure you make it as easy as possible for people to listen to you.

Helping others listen

Following are some tips for helping others to be good listeners. Remember, conversation is a two-way street.

Be interesting for them

Be aware that topics you find fascinating may not fascinate others. This definitely includes talking about your children and your pets. Wonderful and fascinating as they may be to you, they don't necessarily interest anyone else.

Know when to stop

Yes your topic is interesting and you have got everyone listening – just don't overdo it. It is possible to have too much of a good thing.

Speak to be heard

If you are softly spoken people will try and listen in the beginning and may ask you to repeat yourself once or twice, but be warned – after that they will give up. It's just too hard straining to listen to someone who's not making the effort to be heard.

Talk to them not shout at them

If you intimidate the person you are talking to they won't listen. Watch out if you are particularly tall or have a booming voice; you might fall into this category without even realising it.

Be sparing when repeating what others have said

Repeating or paraphrasing the words of others can help you understand and clarify what has been said. Watch out you don't do it too often as it may come across as you simply like to hear your own voice.

You can often spot this happening in meetings, where someone always seems to feel the need to echo the sentiments of someone else, almost as an excuse to speak. It doesn't add anything to the conversation and everyone switches off.

Ask if your advice is wanted before giving it

Giving unsolicited advice is a sure way to stop people listening to you. If people want advice they will usually ask, 'What do you think?' For most of the time, though, people just want someone to listen to them and have empathy with their situation; they don't necessarily want to be told what to do. If you really feel you have a possible solution to their problem, why not find out if they want to hear it first. For example, you could say:

'Would you like me to go through some options?' or 'Would you like some help here?' If they say 'yes', then away you go. If they say 'no', you need to shut up and keep listening. In this instance, don't take their refusal to receive advice personally.

Top Tip: People are more likely to listen to you if you listen to them

---

> *Listening is a need we have; it's a gift we give.* – Michael P Nichols[xii]

MILLER'S LAW

To help with your listening skills, consider the words of Princeton University psychologist George A Miller.

> *To understand what another person is saying, you must assume that it is true and try to imagine what it could be true of.*

In reality what can actually happen is that we do the complete opposite. When someone says something we are far more likely to assume what they said was false rather than true. Then we spend the rest of the time while they are talking working out how to justify our conclusions. Having this justification conversation in your head means it just isn't possible to listen to others so we stop listening and don't hear the full story.

Miller goes on to say,

> *Even if the other person seems crazy or wrong, really listen to him, without judgment, and try to figure out how he could think that way.*[xiii]

Statements such as 'I am sorry I am late for work, the bus was involved in an accident', can prompt a false conclusion, such as 'Susan doesn't like working here, she's often late and I don't believe that anything happened to the bus this morning'. Or being told 'I think your paintings are wonderful' can prompt you to draw the false conclusion that 'Megan's just saying that because she is my brothers' girlfriend.'

And so the conversation goes downhill.

Top Tip: Be open to what others have to say and assume that there is truth and reason behind what they have to say. Your openness will enable you to listen properly to what is being said, allowing you access to the full story, make accurate judgments and potentially learn from that story.
---

chapter five
Conversation
M.O.D.E.™

Understanding everyone's conversation M.O.D.E.™

Do you find some people easier to talk with than others?

Can some people just 'get your back up' without really trying?

Even when you put all your best conversational skills to use you will still find some people easier to talk to than others. It's simply because of your respective conversational styles.

Just like our personalities, some conversational styles are compatible and some styles clash. It is likely the people you have identified as being 'difficult to talk to' have a conflicting conversational style to yourself. Once you understand their conversational style, how they like to communicate and what is important to them, it really becomes quite easy to engage them in productive conversations that help you build up your relationship with them – if you choose to do so.

It enables issues to be tackled without confrontation, reduces misunderstanding and helps build solid relationships you never thought possible.

Of course recognising different personality styles is nothing new. The Greek philosopher, Hippocrates back in 400 BC, recognised the different personalities at play. He hypothesised that we all typically fitted into four main categories. He explained it as something that naturally took place inside of you. According to

Hippocrates it was the fluids that ran through your body that affected how you behaved.

If you had a cold, fast fluid, Hippocrates believed you would be very direct, dominant, decisive and a leader. If you had a fast, warm or hot fluid, so hot and so fast that it might bubble out of your mouth, you would be the kind of person who talks all the time. Or maybe you had a fluid that was warm and slow. In this case you would be family oriented, stable and relational. Finally, you may have had a slow, cold fluid running through you. This made you a thinker, meticulous, a perfectionist who wanted exact details. He named these different personality styles choleric, sanguine, phlegmatic, and melancholy.

It wasn't until the 20th century that Hippocrates work was expanded upon. And today we have numerous personality types, psychometric tests, behavioural types and popular left brain/right brain theories that are regularly used in the workplace. They can help build teams, develop management and leadership skills and recruit new staff. They all lead to a similar conclusion.

We are all different!

And so it follows we all have different conversational styles. What works for one in conversation may not work for someone else. Yet rarely would we consider this when we are in conversation with someone else. We just typically talk the same way we always do and that is where some of our conversations may fall down. Some people prefer to stick to the facts and have a logical, more structured approach to conversation whilst others may prefer more fluid discussions about relationships and emotions. Even the way we deliver our conversations is different. Some of us are softly spoken and more reserved in our delivery whilst others chat away at high speed with their hands frantically accompanying them.

In order to have successful conversations with everyone we meet it is important to be able to adapt our style to suit theirs.

The good news is, underneath our unique qualities and the great diversification in our society we still tend to fall into four main modes that influence our preferred conversational style, just as Hippocrates hypothesised so many years ago. So in order to be able to have a successful conversation with just about anyone all you have to do is understand these four main conversational styles and away you go. Let's take a look at these four styles: Minders, Organisers, Directors and Enthusiasts.

Minders

Minders are motivated by security so they are unlikely to say anything to jeopardise that security or rock the boat. They will avoid arguing for that very reason.

- They can be prone to saying 'yes' too much which can lead to them taking on too much work such as helping friends move, looking after the neighbour's dog and running the school fête.

- They are loyal to their family and their work, so they won't speak out of turn about them and they won't appreciate you doing so either.

- They are very relationship orientated so their conversation will be relationship focused.

- They are very good listeners and counsellor of others; as a result, you may find you are doing more of the talking when in conversation with them.

- They tend to speak softly and at a slower pace and they have more seated conversations.

- They will appear friendly and empathetic because they are!

- They are sincere in what they say and make good eye contact

Organisers

Organisers are motivated by procedures and getting the task done correctly. If they have to participate in the conversation they are happiest if everyone sticks to the facts.

- They dislike being interrupted from their work and will often continue working whilst 'in conversation' with you, not always making good eye contact.

- They get uncomfortable if the conversation turns to relationship issues.

- Like Minders, Organisers tend to talk at a slower, often softer pace.

- They dislike social chit chat and big social events. In many ways they are more comfortable conversing via email, SMS or notes on the kitchen table rather than face to face conversations.

- Organisers are sceptical by nature so don't be surprised when they question what you have to say.

- They can be so involved in their tasks they can forget to talk to you at all. They might come into the office and want to get their PC booted up or come home at night and want to get the dinner on not realising they should say hello first.

Directors

Directors are motivated by power and control and you will typically hear them coming as they go racing by.

- Directors have strong opinions, strong voices and they are comfortable taking the lead in conversations.

- They want immediate results and will often override your conversation to speed things up.

- Their busy minds, filled with multiple tasks, make them poor listeners. They may ask you a question yet not be around long enough to hear the reply.

- They are quick thinkers and talk at a quick pace.

- They are very assertive so will have no hesitation questioning what you are doing or delegating work to you.

- They are too busy for social chit chat and tend to have conversations on the go.

Enthusiasts

Enthusiasts are motivated by social recognition and they are likely to be the social butterfly of a group.

- They love holding court in conversations and being the entertainer.

- They are upbeat and fun loving so their conversation is highly animated and they use their hands to add emphasis.

- They smile a lot and talk with an optimistic slant.

- Enthusiasts love social chit chat and are happy to talk about emotions and relationships.

- They find conversations around facts and figures very dull, in fact they are likely to switch off and find some else to talk to.

- They, like Directors, think quickly and talk at a fast pace with an equally loud volume.

- They are great lateral thinkers although sometimes their conversation can be hard to follow as they jump around from idea to idea.

- They are very persuasive so you can often find it is an Enthusiast that has just talked you into doing something you weren't necessarily that keen on doing in the first place.

With the four conversation styles of Minder, Organiser, Director and Enthusiast, no one style is better or worse than another, just different. In reality we have elements of all four styles within us, although it is typically one or maybe two styles that tend to dominate how we prefer to handle our conversations.

Just stop for a moment and go back over the four styles. Which style resonates the most with you? Which style do you use the most when you are in conversation?

Now think about people you find hard to talk to. What style do you think they prefer to converse in? Can you start to see where the clashes may occur?

So the secret to successful conversations with everyone you meet comes down to just two things:

1. Identify the conversation style of the person you are talking to.
2. Adapt your conversational style to suit theirs.

You don't have to change who you are; you just have to modify your conversation style to complement theirs. It might mean softening your tone or slowing down at bit. You might need to stop waffling and get to the point. Alternatively you might need to up the energy and get some enthusiasm into your voice.

Let me tell you about a couple of people I know to help you get the picture.

Catherine is a classic Minder. She is one of those lovely people that is a delight to have as a friend. Whenever we catch up I have learnt to slow down; this is not a bad thing. There is something quite calming about her so when I allow myself, I find having a conversation with her incredibly calming. She is very thoughtful and caring. It comes across in her voice. There are no hollow promises coming out of her mouth. If we have a social gathering you will easily spot Catherine. She will no doubt be sitting on the sofa, listening to one of our other friends. Her empathy and ability to listen is fabulous. I talk at a much faster pace than Catherine but I have learnt that the best conversations occur when I slow my conversational speed down. I stop racing between topics and stick with one topic at a time, finish it and then go on to something else.

Probably the most important thing I realised I needed to do though was allow Catherine to finish her sentences. It sounds obvious I know, yet half of the population will be like myself, a quick talker (Directors and Enthusiasts). It is a very easy and bad habit to develop. You really do need to take stock of the number of times you actually end up cutting the other person off because you 'perceive' you know what they are going to say. Catherine, like many other Minders, has a lot of wisdom to share.

Charles is an accountant and really fits the conversational style of the Organiser. He has to be one of the most organised people I know and his attention to detail is wonderful. He picks up on things we never would. He has a real passion for his work and he seems happiest when he has his head focused on a computer screen solving some tricky tax problem. There was an advertisement on television a couple a years ago advertising a firm of accountants that are really good at doing your tax returns. The lady on the advertisement had clearly just completed some really taxing problem (excuse the pun). She celebrates this by giving a tiny smile and a very conservative punch in the air with her hand. She then ploughs straight into the next project. Well this is Charles. There are no wild celebrations in his office. He comes across as quite serious. I used to go into his office, which is very neat and orderly, and start off with a bit of a social chit chat. I now realise this isn't what Charles wants. We now forego the social stuff and head straight to the figures and it works well. Charles, like Catherine, is softly spoken and doesn't like to be rushed. Even though we may have saved time dropping the social chit chat, it doesn't mean it is going to be a quick meeting (well not by my standards anyway). I have also learnt with Charles that emails are a great way to communicate. You can just sense if you call him on the phone that he feels interrupted, whereas with emails he typically replies almost instantly. If it works for him, it certainly works for me.

Diana is a very successful business women and a perfect example of a Director. She has built a thriving marketing business basically on her own. She is very driven and always seems to have clear focus on where she is going. She simply exudes energy and whenever we get chance to catch up it's always just for a quick coffee to fit in with the numerous projects she has on the go. She talks very quickly so there's is no chance of me finishing her sentences. I have learnt our best conversations are when I choose to sit back more and let her do most of the talking as much as I may want to 'compete' in the conversation. She is a great person to ask for advice. She can quickly assess the situation and has no problem telling you straight what she thinks. In fact, she can do it without even been asked. At work she is concise with her wording and when the pressure is on she is even more so. It's almost bullet points coming out of her mouth and it certainly gets people into action.

Lewis is an Enthusiast through and through. He is such fun to talk to. He's always the entertainer even if life is throwing him some tough shots. There is always a funny story to it. He is very animated and very loud. He's a tall man with broad shoulders. His hands are always in action when he is in conversation and as a result he regularly knocks over his or someone else's drink. His conversations constantly dart around and you get insight into just how busy his mind is. He has numerous business ideas on the go and is the perfect person to ask if you need to brainstorm an idea. He can come up with so many solutions that it's amazing. The challenge Lewis and I have when we get together is there can be too much laughter and not enough work. The other day we had planned to work on our shared boat, general maintenance stuff. My partner arrived home, several hours later to discover we hadn't actually got round to leaving the house yet. One conversation had lead to another and the rest as they say was history.

As I describe the conversational styles it is probably becoming clear where the clashes can occur.

Minders and Directors

Minders and Directors can clash. Well, clash possibly isn't the right word here. Directors can bulldoze Minders into doing things they don't want to do and they can easily dominate the conversation. Not surprisingly Minders in their quiet way resent being treated like this. Looking at it from the Directors point of view they get frustrated by the fence sitting nature of Minders. 'Why can't they just make a decision,' you can hear them say. 'If they didn't want to do it, why didn't they just say so,' is another.

Organisers and Enthusiasts

Organisers and Enthusiasts clash too. The conservative nature of an Organiser finds Enthusiasts just too 'out there'. You can see Organisers physically recoiling when an Enthusiast loudly enters the conversation with both arms waving. Enthusiasts are very much 'big picture' people. Not only is the way they talk hard for an Organiser to deal with, they always talk concepts and never get into the detail. As far as the Organiser is concerned there is no substance to what they are saying. There are no facts to back up their argument. Conversely Enthusiasts find Organisers challenging to talk to because they are so serious. All they want to do is have their nose stuck in a book or gaze at a computer screen all day. 'Where is the fun in that?' an Enthusiast would say.

Directors and Directors

Directors and Directors can clash too. They have a strong conversational style and will both want to lead the discussion, voice their opinions and win any argument. So if there is ever a fiery discussion around the dinner table it is likely it is between two Directors.

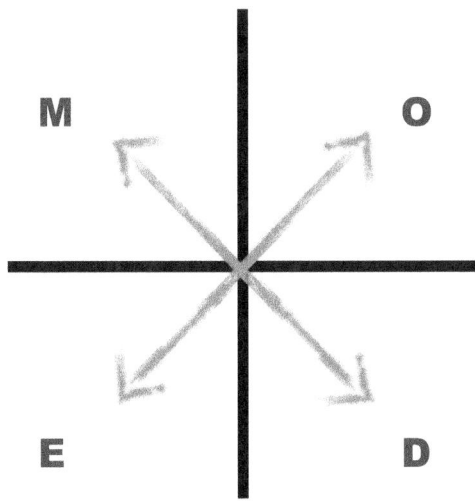

Figure 2: Conversation M.O.D.E.™ and their most common differences

So now you know the main conversational styles. Make a note of the style(s) you are most likely to clash with. This is going to be the style you find hardest to converse with. Think about who you know who uses this conflicting style. Think about what you can do to engage this style and focus first on improving these conversations. Once you have made improvements there, try the next 'challenging' person. If you take a focused step by step approach it will allow you not only to master the skill of style adaptation but also to see the success your changes can bring. Over time you will find the process starts to become an automatic one.

Remember simply by adapting your style to suit the person you are talking to can have a dramatic effect on the conversation. It really does enhance the conversation experience for them. You can quickly get them engaged, make them feel more comfortable, break down any awkward conversational barriers and as a result make your conversations more successful for you

… # chapter six
Building rapport

BUILDING RAPPORT

An oft used phrase of mine when training people in 'Selling is just a conversation™' is that 'People buy people first' and they buy from you because they trust you. They trust you because you have been able to build rapport with them. Essentially rapport is built when the parties involved in conversation perceive they are on the same 'wave-length'.

Conversation in rapport will always bear greater fruit. Following are some excellent techniques, tips, and tricks for building rapport.

Use people's names

Isn't it lovely when a person you don't know that well remembers your name? It makes you feel good, doesn't it? It makes you feel special. When in conversation with others, use the same technique to make them feel special by remembering and using their names.

I know not all of us are great at remembering names – myself included. The best tactic I have found is to say **someone's** name when you're first introduced to them. Then try and drop it into the very next sentence; that way it often sticks. I also think about who might be at a function I am going to attend, and I'll write down the names of people I think might be there and any other relevant information I can think of about them to help jog my memory when I get there.

Because I'm not great at remembering names myself, I try and help others out where I can. When I join a group of people I say my name clearly when I meet them, even if we have met occasionally before. That way it eases the pressure on them to remember my name. I will also introduce myself to the other parties in a conversation, which again reduces the pressure on any people I have previously met. If I can remember how we are connected or when we last met, I will say that too.

Speak their language

Another other great tactic for building rapport in conversation is to use the other person's words when you are following up from what they have said. It not only shows you have been listening to them, but it also shows that you have an acceptance of their statement. Of course, accepting what they are saying doesn't mean you have to necessarily agree.

A classic example of how important this is came to light during a team-building session I was running. John was a manager who liked to do everything himself, and in many ways he was the major contributor to the poor performance of the team. He struggled to let go, and found delegation nearly impossible. As a result, he was overworked and the team as a whole wasn't performing well.

The team-building session was aimed at brainstorming ideas about how the team could improve performance. Joanne, who was a new member of the sales team, was full of energy and enthusiasm and had great ideas on how to get increased performance from the team. One of her suggestions was a 'customer swap' to move around the tricky clients to see if someone else might have more luck with them.

John thought this was a good idea – yet instead of referring to Joanne's idea as 'customer swap', he referred to it as 'client reassignment'. It was almost as if the new wording gave him ownership of the idea. Joanne, to her credit, was not perturbed. She picked up on the phrasing 'client reassignment', and then launched into another idea that her old company employed which they called 'bar analysis treatment' or BAT for short.

Once a month the team would get together for 'BAT time' in either a bar or café to chat casually about problem clients, to look at the best ways to use their marketing material, to discuss sales pitches and to help each other get their deals in. You could see the team nodding in agreement that this would work well for them. They needed some BAT time too.

John picked up on their enthusiasm, yet he referred to the idea as 'monthly sales forums'. What happened to 'BAT time'? Even I felt cheated and I wasn't part of the team! It would have been so easy for John to use Joanne's words – and it would have had much greater impact on both the team and on Joanne. By using different words, even though he was actually embracing the concept, John took ownership of the idea and lost the enthusiasm of the team – as well as losing a chance to praise a team member for her good ideas.

Where possible, when you are referring to something someone else has just said, try and use their words to show you have listened and accepted what they have had to say.

Showing praise and giving feedback

When was the last time you told someone how much you appreciated them, their role, their work?

Hmmm..............

I am sure some of you are able to recently recall something, for most of us though it might have been a while since we actually told someone how much we appreciate them.

> *The deepest craving in human nature is the craving to be appreciated.*
> *William James 1842-1910*

William James was so right when he wrote those words. How great is it when someone makes you feel appreciated for who you are and what you do?

We were called in to help a graphics company with their staff performance reviews. Things had been going really well for the company so much so that more and more work was coming in and the two managers realised everyone needed to increase their effectiveness to cope with the increased demand. They had introduced performance indicators and performance reviews to help address the increasing demand and it was during these performance reviews that things were starting to go down hill.. Instead of boosting morale it was denting it and some staff actually become quite hostile to the process.

As we investigated, the cause of this hostility quickly became apparent. Culturally no one had ever previously received feedback on their performance. They had been left to their own devices for a long time and all thought they were doing OK. (which for all intents and purposes they were). As a result the employees were rather wary about the review process, they weren't sure what the managers were going to say. The managers on the other hand saw the review process as a great opportunity to up skill everyone, so had used the process more as a training session. They spent their time telling staff how they could improve their effectiveness by streamlining their processes and procedures. They had omitted to let the employees know just how appreciated they were and what a good job they were all currently doing. As a result all the employees really heard from their meeting was 'criticism' and so they left feeling demoralised.

The managers were surprised "surely they should have realised they were doing a good job. Surely they know we appreciate the effort they put in?" It was these simple assumptions that caused all the problems. People really don't feel appreciated unless you tell them. They won't know you think they are doing a great job unless you tell them.

The reality was that these two managers were flat-chat keeping their busy company growing. They were racing from project to project, ensuring every detail was correct to keep their clients happy.

The one thing they were forgetting to do was let their employees know how much they appreciated their commitment to the company and to praise them on a job well done. Because these managers rarely gave any positive feedback to their staff it wasn't surprising that their suggestions for improvement were greeted with such a negative response.

> Top Tips: **Everyone** needs appreciation and praise and likes to know what they are doing well, so you should give praise regularly.

There are several things to learn here

1. People really need to feel appreciated for who they are and what they do..

2. Make the effort to tell people regularly how much you appreciate them. Don't assume they will know

3. If you never give anyone positive feedback in the form of appreciation and praise don't be surprised if they aren't open to feedback on how they can improve.

Of course out of work and in our personal lives the same is true. We all have a need to be appreciated. For so many of us appreciation and praise is a rare commodity. And that's not saying we're not doing a good job or that our nearest and dearest don't love us, it's simply that the people around us aren't good at giving positive feedback. And to make matters worse it is often those that are slow to praise us, are quick to point out when we have got it wrong and that is rather irritating to say the least!

> Top Tip: You shouldn't hand out feedback on how someone can improve if you haven't regularly been giving them praise. If you give feedback without praise, don't be surprised if your feedback, no matter how helpful it is, doesn't go down well.

As a general rule you need to be giving at least **four times** as much praise as you do feedback. This applies to your staff members, your partner, your children. Everyone needs to hear about what they are doing well and will stop listening to you if all you can do is criticise their behaviour.

Specific praise

Specific praise is about saying 'well done', 'great job', 'excellent work'. The more specific you can be about what is it the person has done well, the more powerful and believable your statement becomes.

Watch out for throwing out hollow statements around the office or the family dining table. Statements like 'good job everyone', especially if used often, will have little or no meaning to anyone. Praise requires thought from you. You have to first observe the behaviours or attitudes that warrant praise in order for your statement to have real impact.

Here are some examples of good specific praise statements:

'Well done, Jenny, on completing that tricky contract in time.'

'David, you did a great job of staying calm when the neighbour complained about our fence.'

'Your spelling words are lovely and neat, you should be very proud of your work.'

Words such as those below should regularly be falling out of your mouth as you generously give appropriate specific praise.

remarkable impressive gifted wonderful
exceptional *tremendous*
outstanding amazing
super marvellous
terrific
brilliant fabulous
superb extraordinary
fantastic

If and only if you are regularly giving praise should you consider giving helpful feedback.

Helpful feedback

It is far easier to give criticism rather than helpful feedback. After all;

You know……, you can see what they are doing is 'wrong'…..

You know you are in the 'right' to point out the error of their ways.

So you do just that and tell them their errors

Then you are amazed they reacted so badly to your feedback.

What is wrong with 'them'?

A couple of years ago when our son was a toddler and our daughter was just a baby precisely this happened.

My partner kept on leaving the washing machine door open (along with just about every other cupboard door in the kitchen) so I pointed out she should keep it shut. Nice concise feedback I thought.

Now admittedly my timing was poor, my partner had been up most of the night with our young daughter, so she was very tired. The stage of life we were in with two very young children seemed to be one long cycle of washing so I guess I shouldn't have had high expectations from her response. There will be no surprises to hear that, without going into too much detail my feedback didn't go down well at all. In fact it prompted quite a ferocious response that quickly put me back in my box and I have come to realize giving feedback can be potentially quite a dangerous game if you don't do it properly.

First, let us have a look at what helpful feedback is not. It is not criticism. Criticism simply tells the person what they have done wrong or that they have failed to meet expectations. It gives no guidance as to what the person should do in the future. In the end, all it succeeds in doing is making the other person feel bad.

Helpful feedback, on the other hand, gives guidance and direction to the other person as to what they should do to help them improve their performance. It explains why they should take on your suggestions.

Below are some examples of criticism and alternate helpful feedback. Criticism should be avoided and helpful feedback given only when specific praise is regularly given.

Criticism: Your work is shoddy
Helpful feedback: Why don't you have a go at sanding back the edges to reduce the roughness?

Criticism: This room is a mess
Helpful feedback: Before the guests arrive would you put your papers away so that everyone has somewhere to sit?

Criticism: You were really fidgety in that presentation
Helpful feedback: When we are meeting with clients, would you try and rest your hands in your lap so they can focus on what you are saying?

Criticism: Your hair is a mess
Helpful feedback: I have put a brush in the car so when we visit Grandma you can quickly brush your hair before we go in to stop her nagging you.

Criticism: The proposal you wrote was substandard
Helpful feedback: I have emailed you a proposal template to give you a structure to follow. That should make it easier for you to understand our format.

As you can see from the two columns, it takes far less time and effort to give criticism than helpful feedback. Helpful feedback does require more thought. You need to observe the issue then work out what needs to happen to resolve it and state why this should be done.

In my washing machine scenario I should have thought about my timing. I could have easily waited till another day when perhaps my partner was less tired and more receptive. Fundamentally though I didn't explain why I felt the washing machine door should be kept shut. It wasn't just because I like all cupboard doors to be closed, which I do. It was because I was concerned about our son trapping his fingers in the door if he tried to close it himself. At a more appropriate time, I shared my concern with her, to which she replied: "Oh that's a good point, I didn't think of that, why didn't you say that in the first place?..........

The good news is that helpful feedback in conjunction with specific praise is a very effective technique in getting others to change. Your suggestions are far more likely to be taken on board, people are less likely to get defensive and you may even be thanked in the process. So it is well worth making the effort.

The 24-hour feedback rule for partners

In close relationships it is very easy to get niggly with each other and we can get very defensive if our 'nearest and dearest' chooses to find fault with us. What can often happen is this defensiveness turns into attack, and suddenly your partner – who had possibly given you some quite valid feedback – finds themselves under attack as you deluge them with less than helpful feedback. The valid feedback you may well need is conveniently lost in the process.

The 24-hour rule is simple. If you receive helpful feedback, or for that matter criticism, from your partner, you are not allowed to give helpful feedback to them for at least 24 hours and vice versa. This allows the feedback received to be properly digested. If it is helpful feedback that has been supported by lots of specific praise, it is most likely that the feedback will be taken on board. Also, if you happen to have received criticism rather than helpful feedback you have had a chance to cool off and not escalate into your own critical response.

Subject to your personality the 24-hour rule can be a life saver. I have to confess to a personality trait that doesn't naturally receive feedback particularly well, coupled with highly developed skills of persuasion I had an ability to re-frame the helpful feedback such that my partner would always leave the conversation feeling as though the situation was her fault. How frustrating would that be to live with! It was during one such helpful feedback discussion that we came up with the 24-hour rule and it has made a fantastic difference to our communication.

Helpful feedback in close relationships

I find the following tips useful in helping to smooth the process of giving helpful feedback in close relationships.

1. Be specific about the behaviour and distinguish it from the person. It is the behaviour you dislike, not them! Ensure this is very clear.

For example, instead of saying 'You are really messy', be specific in your thinking and distinguish the *behaviour* from the *person*. Perhaps the issue here is that Belinda always leaves her dirty washing on the floor.

If you were to say this to her, although it's specific, it's still likely to raise a defensive response such as, 'No I don't.' Here's where you move on to step two.

> 2. Try using the word 'I' instead of 'you'. It helps the other person understand the impact their actions have on you.

For example, why not try saying, 'I am really frustrated with finding washing on the floor and I am tired of picking it up. From now on only washing that makes it to the washing basket will get washed.'

This statement is clear about how you feel. It is also less confrontational and very directional. You've clearly told others what they need to do to get their clothes washed – and you are more likely to get your desired result.

Be positive

Be positive in what you say, and make an effort to avoid viewing life negatively. When you meet someone for the first time, you want to leave them with a positive impression of yourself rather than them seeing you as a whinger or negative.

We were going to a large award ceremony in Melbourne where there were lots of industry people present that I was keen to network with. Special entertainment had been laid on and we had been given strict instructions not to be late. We had recently had our second child, and were looking forward to going out and leaving the kids with a nanny for the evening. 'Mum' had even borrowed a girlfriend's dress for the event.

The nanny arrived and our young son charged round the apartment in excitement.

Crash!

Our son ran straight into the glass coffee table. Blood poured from his nose. All I could see was cream carpet, cream rug, cream sofa, and so could mum. She whisked him up and into the shower. Finally his nose stopped bleeding. The bathroom looked like a murder scene, but we were going to be late, and the taxi was waiting.

So we ran for the taxi without having time to clean up properly. My partner now had wet hair, smudged make up, a damp dress and would no doubt be feeling queasy as she hates the sight of blood. I thought I should be prepared for the worst. She could get to this function and just decide she doesn't want to participate. Was our evening going to be ruined?

She told me afterwards she made a conscious decision to forget about the accident. She was feeling queasy and knew that just talking about the incident could make her feel faint – so she decided to move on and enjoy the evening without thinking any further about it.

And that is what she did. She was positive to everyone she met, chatting about more upbeat subjects, and I am sure those that met her would have been left with a really positive impression. I thought how different the evening would have been if she had allowed the accident to take precedence. If she had talked about our son's accident I am sure she would have got sympathy, but would it have been a good starting point for meeting someone new? I don't think so.

> Top Tip: When you are meeting someone new, focus on the positives in life and leave the war stories, your complaints, grudges and whinges for another time.

chapter seven
Body language

BODY LANGUAGE

Human beings are visual creatures and we rely hugely on visual cues to assess who people are, and whether we trust them, believe them or like them, simply by how they look and how they hold themselves.

Aware that there has been a great deal of research and books written on the subject of body language you may well wish to speed read, or skip, this chapter. That said, there are some key aspects of what we 'Do' in conversations with our physical form that warrant re-visiting and focusing on if we are to have the best conversations we can.

Your own body language

Once you get into conversation with someone, you will still be relying on their visual cues to get the full meaning of what they are saying or perhaps are not saying. These visual cues combine to form an articulate language of their own and anyone who has observed deaf people signing to each other will have seen how engaging and fluid a visual language can be.

Most of us, though, rarely consider our visual language and how we are communicating visually. Instead we tend to leave it to our subconscious mind to communicate via visual cues. Let me describe some of these visual cues that you may be giving without really being aware of doing so.

- You are in a meeting and someone asks you a tricky question. Without being aware of it, you will suddenly 'find the seat uncomfortable', wriggle to change positions, and stop looking at the questioner. (This visual clue says you're unsure of the answer!)

- You are out shopping and your girlfriend pops into a changing room to try on a dress. She comes out to ask your opinion you think she looks terrible. You suddenly notice you have crossed your arms. (You're either being defensive about what you are going to say ... or you could just be cold!)

- You are in a meeting that is running late and you desperately want to leave. You notice that you have started to tap your fingers or pen on the table. (Your visual cues are saying loud and clear that you want to end the conversation.)

- You are trying to work out your son's tricky homework, and notice that your thumb comes under your chin and your forefinger points up and to the side. (This signals critical evaluation.)

In essence, your body is quite happy having its own conversation with anyone that happens to be watching. Generally this isn't a problem and your natural body language simply adds depth to what you are saying. Where it can become a challenge is when you don't want others around you to know what you are really thinking.

In these instances when there is inconsistency between what you think and what you are saying, your body language and facial expressions can easily give you away. To avoid this happening you need to avoid using negative body language positions in conversation. You also need to develop and constantly use strong, positive body language positions.

Typically negative body language to be avoided:

- Hands covering mouth (when speaking indicates deceit, when listening indicates you don't believe what is being said)
- Scratching your nose (when speaking indicates deceit, when listening indicates that you don't believe what is being said)
- Rubbing your ear (you don't like what you hear)
- Crossing your arms (negative attitude, defensive)
- Tapping pens, fingers, feet or swinging legs (impatient)
- Playing or touching your watch (impatient, or concerned about time)
- Hands behind head when seated (dominance)
- Hands on hips (aggressive or defensive attitude)
- Breaking eye contact (don't want to listen any more)
- Pointing fingers (accusation)

- Leaning away from the speaker and/or crossing your legs away (negative or defensive attitude)

- Slouching in chair (tired, uninterested)

- Hands clenched together (holding back, negative attitude)

- Hands held behind back (superiority).

Typically positive body language to be used regularly:

- Smile to help build rapport

- Shake hands firmly to show you are really pleased to meet the person

- Make good eye contact with the person speaking

- Share your eye contact when speaking with everyone that is listening

- When standing:
  - Turn towards the person speaking, have your arms relaxed and by your sides or held loosely together in front of you
  - When you are talking, feel free to allow your arms to talk too, then let them return naturally to your sides or loosely in front of you
  - Keep your feet hip-distance apart so you are nicely balanced
  - Stand as tall as you can, keeping a strong confident pose

- When seated:
  - Rotate the chair or yourself to face the speaker
  - If you cross your legs, cross them towards the speaker
  - Hand to chin, chin stroking (evaluating)
  - Tilted head (interested)
  - Keep arms open, either resting on the table or resting uncrossed in your lap
  - Sit tall, keeping a strong, confident pose.

Smiling

Smiling is a wonderful tool to use for breaking the ice with people you don't know, to build rapport and make a good first impression. Ensure you smile with your entire face so that your eyes are smiling as well as your mouth. Think about whether or not you smile a lot.

> *'A smile is the shortest distance between two people.'*
> Victor Borge

Some people smile very easily. They are always smiling and they are probably really good at making a positive first impression because their smiles are so welcoming. If you are one of these people then an excellent exercise for you is to practice your straight face. You need a strong straight face for when you want to be taken seriously and when you want others to pay careful attention to what you have to say.[xiv]

On the other hand, some people just aren't natural smilers. You are likely to be very good at delivering more serious information and being very believable. The key area for you to practice is to smile more! Use a big genuine smile with your entire face when you first meet someone to help you make a good first impression and make an effort to smile again and again in the conversation when opportunities arise, such as when someone new starts to speak. Try smiling to encourage them to speak, when someone says or attempts to say something funny, and when it is time to say goodbye and you want to convey how much you have enjoyed the conversation and their company.

The art of consciously transitioning between a warm genuine smile and a serious face in a conversation has a dramatic effect on your message and can really add impact to what you are saying.

Eye contact

Eye contact is one of the best tools you have in terms of a conversational skills kit-bag. Strong eye contact, looking at a person as they're talking, is a key indicator that you are interested in what they are talking about. When you are doing the talking, strong eye contact with everyone listening shows you are confident in what you are saying and also shows that you want to make everyone feel included in the conversation.

Make sure you share your eye contact equally with the group you are talking to and watch no one is missed out, especially those by your side who may be harder to get eye contact with.

Your eyes can pick up on the subtle body language cues that others are subconsciously emitting. This means that even as you are talking you will be able to ascertain how your audience is really feeling and you can then respond appropriately.

> Top Tip: If you want to make a good impression with someone, make your eye contact lasting.

Observing others' body language

We have spent quite some time looking into what you should be doing in terms of your body language and your facial gestures. It is also essential to consciously observe the changes in the body language of others when you are in conversation with them.

Noticing the changes in others' body language tells you much about what they are thinking. You can get to see before they even speak whether they liked or disliked your idea, or whether they are in agreement with you. It confirms whether you are on the right track or whether you need to reframe your position.[xv]

What you are looking for are the adjustments the other person makes to their body language or facial expressions that coincide with your statements. You might be talking to a friend in a café who is relaxed and leaning back in her chair holding her coffee. Then you start telling her about the strange behaviour of your next-door neighbour and suddenly she has leaned towards you (which suggests that she's interested). On the other hand, alarm bells should ring if instead of leaning forward she puts her coffee down, crosses her arms and crosses her legs away from you.

Whatever the reason, if you spot a shift to negative body language, you need to consider what you may have said or done that has potentially caused this shift. Don't ignore it. This change in body language is telling you something and to avoid any potential misunderstandings or conflict it's best to address it straight away. Take it on as your responsibility that you haven't clearly communicated your message rather than assuming that the other person hasn't listened properly. For example, you could say: 'I'm sorry, I'm not sure my point came across as I intended. What I meant to say was ...' Or you could ask them how they feel about the issue you are talking about.

By observing and acting on the silent visual language of others, your conversations will become far more meaningful and productive.

Positive expectancy

A concept that I like to use with my clients is positive expectancy (also known as the Pygmalion Effect). It is the idea that one's expectations about a person can eventually lead that person to behave and achieve in ways that confirm those expectations.[xvi] For example, if I am sitting at a dinner function next to someone who I expect is going to be really boring, they are more likely to be boring.

How does this happen?

It's very simple really. As we discussed previously, we have conversations on two levels. The first is a conscious level where we typically focus on the words we are saying, and the second is a subconscious level which has to do with how we deliver those words and what we do in terms of body language and facial expressions. When we are talking to someone we communicate our expectations of them both consciously and subconsciously. These expectations are received by the other person and as a result they tend to perform in a way that is consistent to the way you expected them to perform.

If you believe you are sitting next to someone who is really boring, even though you don't say as much, your body language, facial expressions and tone of voice will give you away. The other person will pick up on your very low expectations of them. Maybe your smile at introduction didn't appear genuine; you may have broken eye contact too quickly, or perhaps the angle of your chair is the give-away. Whatever the cues you have given them, they are likely to think, 'Well, if he is not interested in talking to me I won't waste my time talking to him,' and as a result they behave just how you expected them to. Conversely if you ask someone to carry out a task and your expectation is that they will carry it out well, they will pick up on the subconscious message that reinforces your belief in them. This will fuel their motivation to do well and as a result they are more likely to do well.

> Top Tip: Think positively of the person you are talking to and you will have a better conversation.

Project confidence

In the same way that positive expectancy can help produce your desired outcome, simply changing your physical position can change how you feel.[xvii]

If you lie down or slouch on a sofa you will feel tired and find it hard to concentrate. Here's an example of how much your position can affect your ability to concentrate.

My partner struggles sleeping so if we are watching television in the evening she will dim the lights and lie down on the sofa, preparing herself to sleep. I, on the other hand, don't have problem sleeping. Unfortunately, what the dim lights and reclining position do to me is cause me to fall asleep within minutes, missing whatever programme I had intended to watch.

So a reclined position is perfect if you want to sleep – and not so good if you are meant to be thinking and alert. If you want to get your brain engaged, you need to sit upright or stand up.

In the same way, if you want to feel confident, you need to put your body in a confident position. Stand tall, push your shoulders back, hold your head up high, uncross your arms and walk with purpose. Next time you walk into a crowded room, change your walk to a really confident one, and you will be amazed by how simply changing how you carry your body changes how you feel and think inside. Others will notice the change, too.

Here are a few simple tips to help you project confidence – no matter how you're feeling inside.

- Stand up straight and walk tall with purpose
- Smile
- Look whoever you are talking to straight in the eye
- Have a firm handshake (avoid crushing the other person's knuckles).
- Keep your voice strong so everyone can hear you.
- To sound authoritative, lower your voice and slow the pace. You will lose the appearance of authority if you race through what you have to say.

Pacing: subconscious rapport building

According to communication experts Joseph O'Connor and Ian McDermott, building rapport with people is all about 'pacing', or mirroring the body language of others. O'Connor and McDermott explain:

> 'Pacing is, in simple terms, adopting similar body positions to that of the person you are talking to. It is not exactly copying – people will think you are odd if you do that. Pacing is taking similar poses to the other person and changing your pose at a similar time to them. Generally, pacing is a totally subconscious exercise. It helps us build rapport on a subconscious level by giving the other party to the conversation a feeling of being listened to, and of you being open to them.' [xviii]

If you are in a pub or bar, try this: just stop and watch what is going on around you. There will be lots of subconscious rapport building happening. For example, you might see a man and woman chatting at the bar. Firstly she leans her arm on the bar and then the next minute the man has his arm on the bar. This is something we do naturally with people we want to build rapport with. The key is to make this more of a conscious act when we want to build rapport with people we might not in reality want as our new best friends.

If you are in a meeting and want to get along with person X, adopt similar body positions, with the exception of closed body language, so if they lean forward to talk about something, you lean forward too. If they lean back in their chair in a more relaxed pose as they chat, then you should adopt a similar pose.

As well as pacing body language you can also subconsciously build rapport by reflecting similar energy levels to the other person. If someone has a slower, more deliberate speech pattern, slow down your own speech pattern. Conversely, if someone talks quickly to get their point across succinctly you should try to do the same.

Once you get the hang of pacing, it can be a really valuable tool to help you calm someone down if they come to you upset or angry. First you should match your pace to their upset pace. Your breathing should become more rapid, your movements more jerky, and your voice louder and clipped. By doing this you are showing them on a subconscious level that you understand where they are coming from. You have got their attention; they feel you are on their wavelength, and that in itself eases some of their tension.

Then, gradually, you can start to lead the other person into a calmer space by slowing down your own breathing, slowing and softening your speech, and reducing your body movements. It does take a little bit of practice, but when you get the hang of it, this is a really effective way of calming others down.

Chapter eight
First impressions

FIRST IMPRESSIONS

Ask a person what they understand by first impressions and they are likely to say it's the assessment we make of someone when we meet them for the first time. And they're right; this is what first impressions are all about.

When we meet someone for the first time we assess whether we like them, whether we should trust and believe them, whether we find them attractive, how smart we perceive they are and how capable they are in the role we see them in. What people probably don't realise or haven't thought about is how automatic this assessment process is. People assess each other every day, from the person serving you at the supermarket checkout to your sister's new boyfriend, the taxi driver, and your new neighbour. When you meet someone new, you don't consciously think, 'Right. I've not met this person before so I should make an assessment of them.' Instead, the assessment happens automatically, without any conscious thought, and incredibly fast.

A 1996 study showed that it only takes us two minutes to form a first impression of someone.[xix] So when you turn up at a friend's barbeque and join a group of new people the 'timer' is on and people are very quickly making an assessment of you without even realising it.

Once the two minutes is up, no matter whether or not you were ready, it is too late. Everyone in the group has already made an impression of who you are. What's worse, it might not be the one you would like them to make.

Now here is the scary thing. Not only do people make first impressions quickly, in just two minutes, but it is also really hard to get people to change their first impression of you once it has been set. We were invited to a barbeque by friends of ours, Pete and Sue. We knew them through work and had often said we should catch up socially and, wonderfully, they had been proactive in organising something.

On the way there my partner and I had a heated discussion over directions. We were running late because the babysitter had been late arriving, so we were already tense, and getting lost just added to our irritability in the car. By the time we arrived we were snappy with each other and walked into the barbeque in a negative frame of mind. Before we had a chance to compose ourselves or get a drink, Pete bounced up to us and introduced us to some of his old school friends. At that moment we had a choice: forget the earlier argument, smile and be engaged in the conversation, or continue to seethe.

It seems an obvious choice doesn't it – you forget the earlier argument and get into the 'party spirit'. And that is certainly what you should do. The trick is in making sure you do it quickly enough to make a good first impression.

Luckily for us Pete is a delightful guy and it is hard to stay grumpy when he is around. My partner and I just looked at each other and smiled and were able to get on with the evening and have some fun. The challenge is if it takes you a while to warm up, the first impression you will leave others with is one of being either quiet, grumpy or tense, and this will last even though the next time you see them you are back to your more social self.

The good news is, according to the study, when people first meet you they are actually quite lenient in their assessment of you. This means you don't have to be exceptional with your first impressions – you just need to avoid making a bad first impression.

If we had walked into the barbeque and were still too irritated with each to make social chit-chat ourselves, yet were able to smile and make good eye contact with the other guests, then the first impression we would have made would still have been okay and people would have been likely to assess us positively.

So why is it that making a good first impression seems so challenging?

Often when we meet new people we are in new surroundings, which is distracting. Most people find that being on unfamiliar ground generates a level of discomfort that can raise our anxiety levels.

Often there is a pressure associated with meeting someone new, for example a new boss who you perceive could make your work life a success or a nightmare, or your child's new teacher who is likely to have a significant influence on how your child will fare at school over the next year.

This associated pressure and the unfamiliar surroundings can distract us and get in the way of making a good first impression. A friend of ours, Anna, demonstrated the impact this self-imposed pressure can have recently. We'd been meaning to introduce Anna to another good friend, Phil. He was looking for a new business venture to invest in and we thought Anna's business would be perfect. We arranged to meet in a city wine bar for a drink. Anna was running late, and by the time she arrived she was not only anxious about meeting Phil but was also very flustered. Needless to say, one of the first rules of making a good impression is to arrive on time!

Anna plonked herself down next to me with her coat still on and still tightly clutching her bag on her lap. She was so anxious that she was very rigid and formal in her conversation, could barely smile, and avoided making eye contact with Phil. It was a disaster.

I chatted to Anna afterwards to see what had happened. It turns out she was so worried about saying the wrong thing that she found that she just couldn't say anything at all. How ironic that the one thing she wanted to avoid doing – making a bad first impression – was the one thing she ended up doing.

This self-imposed pressure is generally what stops us from making great first impressions.

Top Tip: You don't have to be the star of the show to make a good first impression. Be nice, be open and show an interest in others, and most importantly, be yourself.

Dress for success

How you look makes a big a difference to how others perceive and judge you.[xx] It is not simply about wearing your finest clothes, it's about looking at the impression your clothes, hair, make-up and accessories give to others, and asking yourself if they fit with the impression you want others to have of you.

What you wear needs to fit with who you are. If you are really uncomfortable wearing suits, shirts and ties then don't wear them; you will only fidget with the collar and take the jacket off at the first opportunity. Think about the industry you work in, and what is appropriate for that industry in terms of the clothes you wear and the way you groom yourself.

For example, if I was turning up to speak at a financial conference, given the finance industry is known for more conservative dress, I would wear a dark suit with a clean-cut white or striped shirt that would help give me a professional appearance. If I were to turn up at my son's school to help out on a working bee, I would wear old jeans and a shirt with the sleeves rolled up, showing I am ready to get my hands dirty.

A quick and easy tip for making people feel comfortable around you is to take off your sunglasses when speaking with others. Very dark sunglasses or reflective sunglasses, though terrific at keeping out the harsh Australian sun, prevent people from seeing your eyes, making eye contact with you, and being able to read you more clearly. It can be very unnerving talking to someone who is wearing sunglasses, so where possible remove them when in conversation – or buy a pair where your eyes are clearly visible.

Talking of glasses, a friend of mine who is very successful in the corporate world has bought a pair of clear glasses. She is rather young-looking and not very tall, and sometimes felt that her appearance was hindering people from taking her as seriously as she would like. Sure enough, she has found that the glasses give her a more take-me-seriously look. Now people are listening to her more intently when they first meet her. And, in fact, she is right: studies have shown eyeglasses encourage the impression of intelligence! [xxi]

Top Tips: Think about the impression you want to give others. When you dress to go out, consider the occasion and who you are likely to meet. Watch out for those 'comfy' clothes; they might be comfy but they may look rather scruffy!

When you meet someone for the first time, try and think beyond their physical appearance. Don't be swayed too much by the way they look. There could be much more to this person than their outward appearance initially suggests.

Something distinctive

Much to my dismay, we recently acquired a new puppy. My partner was insistent that we needed a replacement after our old dog died. Personally I was enjoying the break from walking and despite my rational arguments about it being easier to go away on holidays, a new puppy appeared and my early-morning walking regime recommenced.

Our new puppy Mango is very distinctive. He is a standard poodle, tan in colour, and the best way to describe him is that he looks like a big walking teddy bear. Everyone stops to talk to us and a typical 20-minute walk around the park can easily take over an hour. We've found we've been opened up to a whole new social experience! The conversations are very easy; after all, we have a clear starting point, the dog.

Now this got me thinking. If you always had something distinctive about you, it would make it easy for others to talk to you as they would have a reference point from which they could start their conversation. My partner uses this technique all the time.

She is forever commenting on someone's unusual earrings, coat, tie, or bag when we meet people for the first time. At first I just assumed that she was really into her accessories – but when I thought about it, she often compliments people on things that are clearly not her style.

The other day we were at an awards dinner that I have to admit was quite dreary. I turned around to hear my partner commenting on the interesting watch her neighbour was wearing. He was an older gentleman who lightened up immensely at the comment. It turned out the watch was his late uncle's. It had been acquired in India after a game of cards, and so a great conversation started between this fellow and my partner about the antics of his late uncle. They had a jolly time and as we were in the car on the way home my partner said to me, 'That was surprisingly good fun, I thought it was going to be so boring.' She sat back into her seat with a contented smile – while I, on the other hand, felt exhausted after a really tiring evening.

> Top Tip: Why not wear something distinctive to help others begin conversations with you, and notice the distinctive characteristics of others to give you a great start into a good conversation with them.

How to make great first impressions

Need some help with you first impressions then follow my five step process:

Step one

Acknowledge the form your meeting pressure takes. You might experience any or all of the symptoms below:

- Monkey-speak such as 'They won't like me', 'I don't have anything interesting to say'
- Increased heart-rate
- Sticky palms

- Blushing
- Churning stomach.

Step two

Disregard your monkey-speak. You can only concentrate on one conversation, so make the effort to have it with the person you have just met, rather than with yourself.

You also need to embrace your physical symptoms. If your heart races or your hands go clammy, make light of them. The less importance you place on them, the less importance they will play in your life.

As part of my role as a trainer, I regularly have to get up and talk to new people. I have trained thousands of people, yet without exception, when I stand up at the start of a new training session I feel my stomach churn, my heart rate increases and my palms go clammy.

I've learnt to silence my monkey, yet the physical symptoms I have never managed to silence. Instead, I just embrace them. Knowing how I feel for the first couple of minutes of a training session (just long enough for the participants to make a first impression assessment of me!), I focus on the participants, and remember that this training is about them, not me.

I also ensure that I'm there with plenty of time to spare and am fully prepared. Even if I have run that particular course several times before, I'll still glance through my notes so I am confident I know what I am supposed to be saying. All of this preparation reduces any pre-course jitters.

In the end, I have learnt that embracing the physical nerves actually helps me give the best 'performance' I can and stops me becoming complacent about my role.

Each time I walk into a room full of strangers, I aim not to take them or myself too seriously. This means that if I do stuff up in those opening minutes I am far more able to laugh at myself and that, funnily enough, is far more likely to endear me to my audience and help in creating a good first impression.

Step three

As you prepare to walk in the room, leave your past and future thought baggage behind at the door and allow yourself to be fully present.

Step four

Walk into the room with confidence, standing tall and strong. Even if you don't feel confident, act as though you are confident. Studies have shown that the way we hold our body affects how we think and what we say, so it is really important that you get your body in a strong position to help the right words come out in the right way.

When you are walking up to meet someone new, walk as if you are delighted to see them. A good trick is to imagine they are a long lost friend you are catching up with. Speed up your pace and walk towards them with purpose.

Step five

Finally, when you are meeting new people, converse:

- Make a conscious effort to turn to look at this person (after all, you want to make a good impression, so the least you can do is turn to face them!).
- Make great eye contact.
- Smile genuinely with your eyes as well as your mouth. A flat smile with just your mouth is not a good look.
- If possible, shake hands. This is a great way of opening up crossed arms and getting people to face each other.
- If you are sitting down, turn to face the other person, and lean forward to show interest.
- Take on the responsibility for getting the conversation going; others will thank you for it.
- Ask questions.
- Listen to their responses.
- Avoid interrupting others. Allow them time to speak.
- Compliment the person you are talking with. Compliments, if not overdone, are a great way of warming people to you.
- Find and focus on the similarities you have with the person you are talking to.
- Be honest and be able to laugh at yourself.

- Focus on positive statements (at least initially).

- Keep your voice strong, and make an effort to breathe evenly so your voice is clear and easily heard (this doesn't mean shout, though!).

- Share observations about everyday life, what was in the news today, the latest movie, book, the food on offer, the room, the speaker – simple things that you might have in common.

- Share your passions and interests.

- Initially let others be the funny ones, or allow them to hold the floor. They will love you for listening to them, and you can take up the conversation shortly.

Great opening comments

- Hi I'm xxxxxx, it is really nice to meet you.

- How do you know (the host).

- How did you find the traffic on the way here?

- How did you spend your day today?

- Who do you know here?

- Your tie/necklace/shirt is lovely – can I ask where you bought it from?

- What did you think of the speech/movie/presentation?

chapter nine
Advanced conversation techniques

Advanced conversation techniques

Avoid killing the conversation dead

Killing the conversation is so easy to do. We've probably all done it – and I have certainly had it done to me. This happens when someone asks you a question and you answer it with a really short answer that leaves the other person nowhere to go. Let me give you an example of two guests at a party:

Sally: 'So, Mitchell, what do you do?'

Mitchell: 'I'm an accountant.'

Sally: 'Oh, so where do you work?'

Mitchell: 'In the city.'

Sally: 'Oh, do you work with the host?'

Mitchell: 'Yes.'

Mitchell's short answers are killing the conversation dead. Here he leaves the questioner, in this case Sally, wondering if root canal therapy on her teeth would be preferable than trying to get this conversation going.

So how can you stop killing the conversation?

Well, it's easy. Simply expand a bit more on your responses so that the other person has some more information to work with to get the conversation going.

Let's look at this example again and see how Mitchell could have improved his responses.

Sally: 'So, Mitchell, what do you do?'

Mitchell: 'I'm an accountant for a legal firm in the city, just down by the train station.'

Sally: 'That sounds handy, do you travel in by train?'

Mitchell: 'Yes I do, it works well most of the time and I get time to read, which is always a treat.'

Sally: 'Oh, I love reading too, what are you reading at the moment?'

As you can see, just by giving a little bit more information in your response it gives the other person more information to work with and enables them to easily keep the conversation progressing.

In many situations where you are meeting people you are likely to be asked 'Where do you work?' or 'What do you do?' Think about the response your want to give. Ask yourself what sort of impression you want to give. How are you going to make your response interesting, so it enhances the conversation rather than killing it? Being prepared can really help your conversations get off to a flying start.

Move out of your comfort zone

Tracey and I have no family in Australia so we catch up with friends rather than family. Our friends typically have a similar background, are of a similar age, and many have children who are of a similar age to our children. Even the people we work with are mainly of a similar demographic. Our catch-ups are easy; we have much to talk about, and much in common. What I have noticed, though, is that not having family here has stopped us in particular conversing with people from different generations such as baby boomers, teenagers and older adolescents.

We just don't have those family functions that you used to dread because you knew boring Auntie May and your super-competitive cousin John were going to be there. Yet now I miss those wonderful opportunities to catch up with the different generations. Each generation has something to offer to a conversation; they can add a different perspective to your life. We recently had my nephew and his friend to stay for a couple of months. They were both nineteen years old. Superficially they seemed easily distracted by the sports channel on the television and their desire to keep in touch with what was happening with the English soccer. Once you got past that and got them engaged in conversation, though, they had some really interesting political views that prompted wonderful discussion – and they also introduced us to a brilliant local comedy scene that we simply weren't aware of.

Aside from the age difference, there is also the cultural divide. People have a tendency to spend their time with people from the same or a similar background to themselves – yet so much more can be learnt when you open up a conversation with someone from a different background. Remember the two Iraqi taxi drivers I met earlier on? Just making the effort to talk to someone outside your usual circle can be an incredibly enriching experience.

So move out of your comfort zone and talk to those that are different. You never know what you'll learn!

Timing your conversation

Choosing when to have a conversation, particularly if it involves giving helpful feedback, is a really important decision and if you want to get your point of view across successfully you need to get the timing right.

Avoid difficult conversations just before lunch when the other person may be hungry and find it hard to concentrate, or late at night when the other person is tired and ready for bed.

Things to consider before diving into conversation can include:

- What is going on in their life at the moment? Is now a good time for them?
- Will they be able to listen, or are there likely to be too many distractions around them?

Family members that have just walked in the door from a busy day at the office or school are not going to be open to a discussion on tidiness. They want to put down their bags, maybe change clothes and have a bit of quiet time first.

Likewise, if you are actually busy doing other things, it's not a good time to ask someone a question. If you have asked a question, you need to stop what you are doing and be prepared to listen to the other person's answer. Asking your children how their day at school was will be seen as meaningless if you then head straight into the laundry.

Timing applies to telephone conversations as well. It might be a great time for you to talk, but what about the person you are calling? Are they trying to put their kids to bed, or perhaps just dashing to work because they live in a different time zone?

The other weekend my partner and I had a very productive Saturday morning. My partner sorted out our children's bedrooms and I restructured our filing system. It was late that night and we were tucked up in bed reflecting on our successful day when I started to explain the filing system to my partner. She started laughing – I guess it was pretty funny talking about filing – so I laughed too. I continued to explain the finer points of our new greatly improved filing system. It was then that she stopped laughing and just stared at me. It eventually dawned on me that my timing was perhaps a little off. Filing does not interest my partner at the best of times, so as bedtime conversations go it was probably one of my poorer attempts.

> Top Tip: If you want your conversations to have maximum impact, ensure you get the timing right.

Location and distractions

Having your conversation in the right place is just as important to its success as having it at the right time. Some locations are better than others to stimulate good conversation. The key issues are the distractions a location brings, such as noise, people, traffic, computers, email, telephones and video screens. Loud restaurants, where you have to shout at each other, are not good places to try and resolve marital difficulties, and common workspaces where the entire office can hear are not appropriate places to give helpful feedback to a staff member on their performance. Equally, there is nothing worse than trying to have a conversation with someone who has been drawn to the television that is on in the background. You might have something really important to say but the advertisement for beer or shampoo seems to win in keeping their attention.

> Top Tip: Good conversation is best without distraction, so choose your location to suit the purpose of the conversation.

'A single conversation across the table with a wise person is worth a month's study of books'
– Chinese proverb

Presentations: conversations with many

Everything we have talked about so far applies just as well to presenting to large groups as it does to a one-on-one conversation. In fact the most important thing to remember about presentations is that they are just a conversation. You just happen to be having a conversation with many.

A managing director had called us in to polish both his presentation skills and those of his team members. The managing director is a very likeable man, easy to talk to and very approachable, yet when it came to presenting he would turn into a very stiff, cold, static person. I asked him what was going on – he had great conversation skills that he just didn't use when he was standing up front.

He confessed that he had always feared presenting and even with all his experience, his fear hadn't gone away. I asked him how he felt about having conversations with people instead of presenting to people. 'Oh,' he said, 'I am fine with conversations.'

I changed my tack. 'Okay,' I said, 'then let's not talk about presenting anymore – let's talk about having conversations with many.' So we dropped his formal jacket, we even sat him on the edge of the desk and got him to chat to the audience as he would do if it were a one-on-one conversation. The transformation was astonishing.

> Top Tip: Change how you view the situation and you can change how you handle it.

Tips for successful presentations

- Practice beforehand, then practice again!
- Watch out for and manage your monkey. Your internal dialogue can be very off putting when you are standing up in front of an audience.
- Share your eye contact with the room. If possible, make good eye contact with everyone in the room. Make a point of looking at one person for three to five seconds then

moving on to someone else. If you are in a large room or auditorium, try and make eye contact with the different areas of the room so everyone feels included.

- Use PowerPoint as a tool to enhance your presentation – but it shouldn't *be* your presentation.

- Make sure the key message for each PowerPoint slide is clear. If there isn't a clear message, pull the slide.

- Less is more when it comes to slides, so pull all that excess information off the slide. You can always have it in an appendix or handout.

- Avoid hiding behind or clinging on to lecterns. Where possible, get rid of them altogether.

chapter ten
Other forms of conversation

TECHNOLOGY AND CONVERSATION

Technology is wonderful, it allows us to instantly converse with people where ever they are, whether on the other side of the world, in a meeting or just down at the beach. We can talk on the phone or chat via email and SMS. All are great forms of communication providing they are used properly.

Telephone communication

Telephones – some people love them and can chat on the phone for what seems like days, while others see them as a necessary evil.

When you're on the telephone you lose the visual component of the message (unless, of course, you have a video phone). So the person on the other end, instead of watching your body language, now pays heavy attention to your tone of voice and the emphasis you place on different words. This will require more work from you to make sure you are not misunderstood.

Now I always thought I was good on the phone until my partner gave me some 'helpful feedback' to the contrary. She pointed out she could tell when I was doing other things like reading and responding to emails and this distractedness didn't make her feel appreciated. The tapping of the keyboard was a bit of a give away admittedly, although what she pointed out was more a distracted tone to my voice and poor timing of my responses indicating I wasn't listening properly. I have spent ages trying to master 'multi processing' whilst on the phone and yet my Tracey can pick it every time. As she rightly points out, if you are too busy to talk either don't pick up the telephone in the first place or be honest with the caller that you can't talk for long to avoid 'sham' conversations which I have discovered get you no where.

The different conversational modes use the phone differently too. Let's look at some typical behaviours.

Minders where possible will always answer their phone (it would be rude not too). They will be warm with their greeting whether they are the caller or the receiver and they will ask you how you are and listen patiently to your response. Minders are quite happy to chat on the phone.

Organisers are not big fans of the telephone, so when the phone rings they will often let it go to voice mail. If they do pick up the phone their tone won't necessarily be welcoming, if anything their tone will indicate you have interrupted them, which of course you have. Organisers use the telephone sparingly and if they do it is typically to get more detail on what they are working on.

Directors have a very pragmatic view of the telephone. They mostly use the phone to give orders or make an arrangement. They get straight to the point and are on and off the phone quickly. They are likely to answer the phone simply by giving their name so be prepared to jump in quickly.

Enthusiasts are happy to be on the phone and have a chat. They will normally pick up the phone when it rings, often delighted to have someone to talk to. Even without any visual cues you can "hear" enthusiasts smiling down the phone and you can sense their arms are still waving around in the background.

To ensure you get your message across, here are some tips:

- Before calling the person, think about who you are calling. What is their Conversation M.O.D.E.™? How can you adapt your style to match theirs?

- Think about what you want to say, and what the mood of the conversation is likely to be. How would you greet this person if it was a face to face meeting?

- The expression 'smile before you dial' is a good tip to remember for most conversations. Smiling helps add warmth to your voice, which is a good opener to the conversation. Don't forget to put that smile on when you are ending the conversation, too, so the other person is left with a positive tone. (Very important when talking to Minders and Enthusiasts)

- Sit upright, especially if you're a mumbler or if you speak in a bit of a monotone. You need to be able to get air into your lungs so you can deliver the appropriate message.

- If you want to feel and convey a more assertive tone, stand up. It will change how you speak on the phone and help you when in conversation with Directors and Enthusiasts.

- Use gestures to get your point across. They are not for others to see, but they will help you add appropriate emphasis to the message as well as getting the emphasis on the right words. Interestingly I probably use bigger gestures on the phone than I do face to face.

- Avoid being distracted. Just because the other person can't see you doesn't mean they don't sense that you are not concentrating on the conversation.

> Top Tip: When on the phone, just think about what you would do if the person were present in the room and behave accordingly.

Eat-and-dial

Drinking and eating while on the phone is another interesting topic. I've heard people insist that others can't tell if you're munching or sipping away while you talk. But as far as I see it, this is the equivalent of going out to dinner with someone, picking up your wine, standing up and moving so you are right next to the person's ear, then taking a drink. Would you do that face to face? No! So don't do it on the phone.

Answer or prompt return

Make sure you answer your phone when it rings, or ensure you've got voicemail with an appropriate set up, so that you can return calls at a more convenient moment. Not having phone calls picked up, or returned, leaves people feeling unheard and ignored, just as if you weren't listening to them in a conversation.

Taking notes

Often during phone conversations, especially work phone calls, people will say things that you really need to make a note of. Now we all like to think we are able to multi-task and write and talk at the same time, but in reality it is very tricky.

Ideally, we need to stop talking and listening, make our notes and get back to the conversation. In a face-to-face situation this tends to happen quite smoothly, because as you jot the information down the other person sees this and either slows down or stops until you engage eye contact again, signaling that you are ready to listen once more. On the telephone the other person simply assumes you are listening and has no idea you are trying to make notes. The best thing to do is to let them know what you are doing. If you say, 'That's a great point, John, just let me make a note', the other person will stop and let you do just that. You then need to let them know you are ready to listen once more 'Okay, you were talking about ...' Or, 'Thanks for that'.

Showing you understand

Let's have a look at a situation where someone is explaining something to you. It might be quite involved or detailed, requiring you to do *most* of the listening and them to do *most* of the talking. In a face-to-face situation as they deliver their message you are nodding, smiling or making appropriate facial gestures to indicate to the other person that you understand what they are saying. Even on the phone you will probably still be nodding – the trouble is that they can't see you, so they don't know whether you understand them or not. If they are not getting any response from you they may even ask 'Are you still there?'

To avoid this and to ensure the other person knows you are keeping up with the conversation and understand their points, you need to verbally acknowledge their statements with short expressions. Saying things like 'Yes', 'I get it', 'Uh huh', 'Okay' indicates to them that you are listening and that they should continue. At various points you might even want to clarify your understanding by repeating the key points: 'Okay, just so I can clarify my understanding of X ... '

Of course if you don't understand what they are saying or if you disagree with them, you need to speak up.

Written conversations: email and SMS

Having looked at the reliance we place on body language, facial expressions and tone of voice to get across the true message in our conversations, you won't be surprised to hear that the written word is often misunderstood.

Emails, SMS messages or notes on the kitchen table can often cause quite a stir. I'm sure you've seen it happen: a situation blows up where you meant one thing in your written message, but the response generated shows that it was interpreted quite differently.

In a 1996 study, psychologists Justin Kruger and Nicholas Epley showed why emails are so frequently misunderstood. Their study found that people overestimate their ability to convey their intended tone – be it sarcastic, serious or funny – when they send an email. They found that people also overestimate their ability to correctly interpret the tone of messages that others send to them.[xxii]

'Of course there's nothing new about text-based communication; people have been writing letters for centuries,' Kruger and Epley explain. 'But what's different in this medium is ... the ease with which we can fire things back and forth. It makes text-based communication seem more informal and more like face-to-face communication than it really is.'

So what should you do if you are a fan of SMS, emails or notes? According to this research, the answer is simple. If you are just communicating content or fact such as work information, the location of a meeting place, or someone's telephone number, then email and SMS work just fine. If there is a tone or emotion to your message, then you are far better just picking up the phone or seeing the person face to face if at all possible.

As an exercise, consider the following statements that could be sent via SMS, email or kitchen table note. See if you can put a positive or negative tone to them

'Thanks!'

'Your dinner is in the oven.'

'I am not going out tonight.'

'Your report has been amended.'

Tips for written communication

When using written communication, keep the following tips in mind.

- Be clear on your call to action.

- Be concise.

- Be aware your email may be seen by others and may not be confidential.

- Using all capital letters indicates that you are yelling. Keep capitalised words to a very minimum.

- Always proofread what you've written. Watch out for a tone that may have inadvertently slipped in – frustration, anger. Try to make your message sound as neutral as possible.

- Use the subject line to increase the likelihood that your email is read and not treated as spam.

- Stick to one point per email.

- If necessary, clarify who you are and why you are writing, so that you are up front with your intentions.

- Consider who you are writing to. How technical are they? Ensure you use appropriate language.

- Consider how you present the email. Avoid fancy fonts as many won't translate onto other computers. Do use bullet points and spacing to make your points clearer.

- When receiving emails, keep your focus on the key message rather than trying to work out the intent of the sender.

Conclusion

So there you have it. Some personal musings on 'the art of conversation'. I trust you have got some value from reading it. For me, success in life; financially, emotionally, spiritually, and physically, comes down to people and the relationships we forge with each other throughout conversations.

The relationships we enjoy with our children, friends, colleagues, customers, and family are what define our experience during our journey of life. If you are not getting what you want from those all important relationships, take stock. Look in the mirror and ask yourself if it is what you SAY | THINK | DO that is getting in the way.

As you take stock, what might you choose to do differently from this moment on? Take a moment and decide to take action. What new habits of behaviour or thought would you like to develop? The rewards are well worth it, one can never stop learning improved conversational skills.

We would love to be in conversation with you so why not visit our websites and start a dialogue and remember, it is all ... Just a Conversation™.

Focused on the capability development of sales leaders, Hugh Gyton & Associates recognise the need to deliver programs that drive behavioural change to the conversations people choose to have in order to improve organisational performance.... in sales process, leadership capability, or the relationships (both personal and commercial) that we all enjoy.

Known for their leadership development work in large corporates working with senior executive roles Hugh Gyton & Associates also has the reputation of connecting effectively across all levels of a company to be a catalyst for positive organisational culture shifts.

Hugh Gyton & Associates delivers Conversationomics™ so you connect more, engage more, inspire more, and earn more.

www.hughgyton.com

Whether you are a man working with women or a woman working with men, you'll love 'Talking Genders'. 'Talking Genders' sheds brilliant light on the different ways men and women communicate. It explains so much about the daily communication challenges that play out in the workplace that get in the way of effectively working together.

Talking Genders helps men and women make their business conversations work and has the capacity and flexibility to work with organisations in a number of formats; from one on one coaching for key individuals, workshops for target groups and/or keynotes, webinars to address a wider audience. This 'pick and mix' approach allows you to select the right solution for your organisation. The solution can be a standalone initiative or run as part of internal program.

www.talkinggenders.com.au

Endnotes

[i] Mehrabian, A 2007, *Nonverbal Communication*, Transaction Publishers, Piscataway, NJ.

[ii] Mehrabian, A 1971, *Silent Messages: Implicit Communication of Emotions and Attitudes*, Belmont, CA.

[iii] 2003, *Cambridge Advanced Learners Dictionary*, Cambridge University Press.

[iv] Freud, S 1949, *An Outline of Psychoanalysis*, Norton, New York.

[v] Cappella JN and Palmer MT 1990, 'Attitude similarity, relational history and attraction: The kinesic and vocal behaviours', *Communication Monographs*, Vol. 57, pp. 161–83.

[vi] Baron RA and Donn B 2000, *Social Psychology*, ninth edition, Allyn and Bacon, Boston.

[vii] Gordon RA 1996, 'Impact of ingratiation in judgements and evaluations', *Journal of Personality and Social Psychology*, Vol. 71, pp. 54–70.

[viii] Orpen C 1996, 'The effects of ingratiation and self-promotion tactics on career success', *Social Behaviour and Personality*, Vol. 24, pp. 213–14.

[ix] Carlon NR and Buskit W 1970, *The Science of Behaviour*, Allyn and Bacon, Boston.

[x] Carlon NR and Buskit W 1970, *The Science of Behaviour*, Allyn and Bacon, Boston.

[xi] Beckman HB and Frankel RM 1984, 'The effect of physician behaviour on the collection of data', *Annals of Internal Medicine*, Vol. 101, pp. 692–6.

[xii] Nichols MP 1995, *The Lost Art of Listening*, The Guildford Press, New York.

[xiii] Miller G 1980, 'title', *Psychology Today*, Vol. xx, pp. xx. [pls add missing details.]

[xiv] Krull, DS and Dill JC 1998, 'Do smiles elicit more inferences than do frowns?', *Personality and Social Psychology Bulletin*, Vol. 24, pp. 289–300.

[xv] Pease A 1985, *Body Language*, Camel Publishing Company, Avalon, NSW.

[xvi] Brehm SS and Kassin SM 1996, *Social Psychology*, Houghton Mifflin, Boston.

[xvii] Satir V 1988, *The New Peoplemaking*, Science & Behavior Books, Mountain View, CA.

[xviii] O'Connor J and McDermott I 1996, *Principles of NLP*, Thorsons, London.

[xix] Forgas JP, Williams K and Hippel W von 2004, *Social Motivation: Conscious and Unconscious Processes*, Cambridge University Press, New York.

[xx] Hatfield E and Sprecher S 1986 *Mirror Mirror ... The Importance of Looks in Everyday Life*, SUNY Press, Albany, NY.

[xxi] Terry RL and Krantz JH 1993, 'Dimensions of trait attributions associated with eyeglasses, men's facial hair and women's hair length', *Journal of Applied Psychology,* Vol. 23, pp. 1757–69.

[xxii] 1996, 'missing article title', *Journal of Personality and Social Psychology*, Vol. 89, No. 5, pp. 925–36.

Keep the conversation going and visit

www.hughgyton.com

www.ingramcontent.com/pod-product-compliance
Lightning Source LLC
Chambersburg PA
CBHW050123020526
44112CB00035B/2364